TEACHING FROM A MULTICULTURAL PERSPECTIVE

SURVIVAL SKILLS FOR SCHOLARS

Managing Editor: Peter Labella

Survival Skills for Scholars provides you, the professor or advanced graduate student working in a college or university setting, with practical suggestions for making the most of your academic career. These brief, readable guides will help you with skills that you are required to master as a college professor but may have never been taught in graduate school. Using hands-on, jargon-free advice and examples, forms, lists, and suggestions for additional resources, experts on different aspects of academic life give invaluable tips on managing the day-to-day tasks of academia—effectively and efficiently.

Volumes in This Series

This book was purchased with funds from the George Gund Foundation for the curriculum inclusion project Apr 8, 1997. C.E. Canavan

SURVIVAL SKILLS

TEACHING FROM A MULTICULTURAL PERSPECTIVE

HELEN ROBERTS

JUAN C. GONZALES

OLITA D. HARRIS

DELORES J. HUFF

ANN M. JOHNS

RAY LOU

OTIS L. SCOTT

SAGE Publications
International Educational and Professional Publisher
Thousand Oaks London New Delhi

For information address:

SAGE Publications, Inc.
2455 Teller Road
Thousand Oaks, California 91320
E-mail: order@sagepub.com

SAGE Publications Ltd.
6 Bonhill Street
London EC2A 4PU
United Kingdom

SAGE Publications India Pvt. Ltd.
M-32 Market
Greater Kailash I
New Delhi 110 048 India

Printed in the United States of America

Library of Congress Cataloging-in-Publication Data

Main entry under title:

Teaching from a multicultural perspective / authors, Helen Roberts
... [et al.].
    p.   cm.—(Survival skills for scholars; v. 12)
    Includes bibliographical references.
    ISBN 0-8039-5613-4.—ISBN 0-8039-5614-2 (pbk.)
    1. Multicultural education—United States / 2. Education, Higher—
United States. 3. Curriculum planning—United States.
I. Roberts, Helen. II. Series.
LC1099.3.T435 1994
370.19'6—dc20   94-13647

96 97 98 99 00 01 10 9 8 7 6 5 4 3 2

Sage Production Editor: Diana E. Axelsen

Contents

Introduction

You don't need to be a rocket scientist or a sociologist to recognize that our higher education institutions are undergoing profound change, driven primarily by the students who choose to attend. The purpose of this book is to explore approaches that can lead to more successful teaching and learning in today's multicultural college or university classroom. We are writing this book because there are some exciting new developments in college teaching that address the diversity and the changes in our institutions, and we want to share them with you.

As you will see in our biographies, we have walked many different pathways through education, and we see the subject of this book from many different perspectives. We are professors of government, social work, ethnic studies, and linguistics; administrators in student affairs and academic affairs. We are African American, Anglo American, Asian American, Chicano, and Cherokee. We are many voices, but we are writing one book together, in the first person, in an attempt to convey to you, our colleagues, our unified belief in the following:

❶ We believe that the responsibility for responding to diversity belongs to each and every member of the faculty and that each faculty member and each student, in every college and department, can make a significant contribution to the multicultural environment of the campus.

❷ We believe that it is important to empower faculty to address diversity by providing concrete ideas, strategies, and examples; and by pointing you toward the resources that will help you do this on your campus.

❸ We are convinced that approaches that benefit culturally diverse students also benefit mainstream students and the campus as a whole. Meaningful contact between faculty and students, active student involvement in learning, and a curriculum enriched by multicultural perspectives are good for all students.

❹ We hope that this volume will help to build bridges—between faculty and students, between new faculty and old-timers, and between the students themselves—as we all work together to meet the challenges of diversity in our multicultural institutions.

This book is organized around seven topical aspects of teaching in a multicultural context. Chapter 1 challenges you to think about how the cultural backgrounds of your students relate to their educational goals and achievement and describes six things that every faculty member can do to help weave diversity into the fabric of the campus. Chapter 2 provides you with tools for developing a profile of diversity on your campus, getting reacquainted with your students at the department level, and setting the stage for student success in your department and in your major. You'll get into the classroom in Chapter 3 with five classroom skills you can develop in order to be more effective with diverse students, along with a personal professional development approach to acquiring those skills. Chapter 4 helps you to incorporate multicultural content in your courses, with practical information on how to develop goals related to diversity, use an integrative approach to curriculum change, stimulate faculty collaboration in the change process, and identify resources for getting started.

Teaching strategies for the linguistically and culturally diverse classroom are presented in Chapter 5, with a four-pronged approach including: needs assessment, varying pedagogical techniques, modeling processes and products, and integrating evaluation methods throughout the course. Chapter 6 deals in depth with the challenges of assessment in the multicultural classroom and contains guidelines for using structured peer feedback, daily learning logs, learning files, portfolios, and minicapstone experiences. Then Chapter 7 "brings it all back home" with a heartfelt discussion of what we are all about—teaching the next generation of students to love learning—and provides the keys to developing effective mentoring relationships with our diverse students.

Throughout this book, there are checklists, charts, surveys, questionnaires, and similar devices we have used on our campuses. There are also lots of examples and case studies from our own experience. These are yours to use if they are helpful to you. At the end of each chapter, you will also find a listing of references that we have found particularly useful in developing multicultural approaches.

We have tried to write as if we were sharing our experiences with colleagues at a faculty colloquium. As you read the chapters, you will come across some variability in the terminology we use—even some disagreement among us about the exact way to treat a given situation. Please don't let this variability distract you. It reflects the diversity of our experience and the dynamic state of educational and cultural change to which we have become accustomed in California.

We consider ourselves fortunate to be working in the California State University system today, where the vibrant mix of students challenges us to stretch ourselves as faculty, to teach ourselves to be better teachers, and to expand knowledge in our disciplines into multicultural dimensions.

Last year, nearly one-third of the 55,000 students who received bachelor's degrees from the 20 CSU campuses were ethnic or racial minority students. We are very proud of our role in the education of these American leaders of tomorrow.

Through them, we have begun to reap the immeasurable rewards of addressing diversity in the classroom, and we hope that you will too.

JUAN C. GONZALEZ
OLITA D. HARRIS
DELORES J. HUFF
ANN M. JOHNS
RAY LOU
HELEN ROBERTS
OTIS L. SCOTT

1 | Once You Accept, Then You Can Teach

JUAN C. GONZALEZ

Over the past 25 years, I have been part of America's higher education community. My experience has been as a student, graduate assistant, faculty mentor, and administrator. In every role in which I have participated, I have had incredible successes and failures. A significant and at times overshadowing influence has been the culture, language, and set of experiences that I brought to higher education. Certainly, because I was the first in my family to attend college, I was missing the counsel of parents who had preceded me into the university and understood my journey through academe.

I had always assumed that I had not been encouraged to attend a university because very few Chicanos considered postsecondary education a viable option. My perception as an 18-year-old was that "Chicanos do not go to college." In fact, my K-12 educational experience did not prepare me for my freshman year in college. In an experience that has been affirmed by many other minority students, my high school counselor clearly counseled me not to proceed into higher education, but instead advised me regarding the wonderful opportunities of a military career.

My counselor did not share or explain to me how my low reading ability would have implications for my long-term career goals. Instead, I was only advised to reconsider my desire to attend a college without knowing why I had been redirected. The counselor was not far off base. He had made an accurate assessment as to my potential academic success in a university: I failed my first semester in college due to my sixth-grade reading level.

Reentry and eventual success in my undergraduate studies were primarily due to a set of very special programs. These federally funded programs were specifically designed to assist and encourage students like myself to attend and succeed at a university. The programs referred to as the federally funded Trio programs included Upward Bound, Student Support Services, and Talent Search. These programs literally advocated and secured my admission into the university and subsequently taught me how to read. (The legislative framework for the Trio programs can be found in the Higher Education Act of 1963, as amended, Title IV, Subpart 4.)

This short account is presented only to depict my early experiences and my own set of circumstances upon entering higher education. The fact that I was the first member of a poor, Mexican-American family to attend college and that I started out with an extremely inadequate academic preparation is not unique. Many other poor students, regardless of race, culture, or academic preparation, have succeeded in college. However, only in the last 25 years have Latinos and African Americans been participating in higher education in greater numbers.

My entry into higher education was directly attributable to the 1960s civil rights movement and the federally funded programs designed to enhance the number of minority students entering college. The reality of current educational efforts is that, all too often, "special programs" are still the principle means by which institutions of higher learning are preparing diverse populations for admission to higher education. Although my particular experience some 25 years ago is perhaps explainable, an almost identical situation exists today for many minority students.

As a young Chicano freshman, I stepped into the "ivory tower" environment and immediately felt marginal. There was a distinct feeling that I was some type of liability to the institution. As an entering freshman, I may not have possessed a college-level reading ability, but it was rather simple to detect both the explicit and implicit messages transmitted to me. My language, culture, and experiences were not valued. Even today, students are expressing feelings of isolation, marginality, and a general lack of belonging similar to what I experienced in my undergraduate days. And, as I speak to minority staff, faculty, and students, there is consistent agreement that many things have not changed.

Just a few years ago I had an experience with an entering freshman. This particular student stands out in my mind because he believed he did not belong in an institution of higher learning. In essence, he felt as I did some 25 years ago: that his language, culture, and experiences were not valued.

Ricardo was an extremely bright Mexican American student who was excited yet apprehensive about beginning his freshman year as a pre-med major at a major university. Ricardo's savings from his summer jobs and a financial aid package made it possible for him to attend school. During my first encounter with him at a freshman orientation program, he apologized to me for his parents' unwillingness to participate in the parent part of the orientation. He told me that he was totally "on his own" and that his parents would not be able to assist him financially nor be able to visit him.

After his first week in the residence halls, Ricardo visited me and expressed some concerns. His roommate arrived on campus with a computer, a color television, bookcases filled with reference materials, posters, a stereo system, and great clothes. The only things Ricardo had brought to the dorm room were his textbooks, modest clothing, and a free poster he picked up at the bookstore. Ricardo was anxious about attending the

President's Freshman Reception without a suit or a sports coat to wear; he didn't own either one.

In his first freshman English class, the instructor asked the students to describe their summer vacations. While other students talked about their travels backpacking through Europe, Ricardo described how he had never been out of Los Angeles County. In his communications class, the instructor used Ricardo as an example of "someone" with a nontraditional accent. These experiences made Ricardo feel as though he did not belong. He began to take a serious look at whether or not he had made the right decision to attend a university at all.

Eventually, Ricardo graduated and went on to complete medical school. His success, however, was to a large extent dependent on his ability to find individuals who were willing to help him interpret, analyze, and maneuver through a system that was, and still is, steeped in elitism, process, rules, and complicated traditions. Ricardo's experiences are not uncommon.

What, then, can we do to help students like Ricardo feel as though they belong, to help them succeed in higher education? How can we communicate to our colleagues the appropriate methods of dealing with a diverse student body? Perhaps the unmistakable truth is that no one simple rule or technique will provide us with a panacea for change.

What to Say to Our Colleagues

Many faculty today are engaged in extremely difficult dialogues regarding the issues of diversity, plurality, multiculturalism, and multilingualism. It is my belief that one of higher education's implicit goals is that of creating homogeneity—in essence, to maintain the status quo and to select out those who do not "fit."

I have witnessed, firsthand, at the University of Illinois, Urbana, Champaign, University of Texas at Austin, University of California at Los Angeles, and at my current institution, California State University at San Bernardino, incredible tension once these topics are brought forward for discussion. Fear, anxiety, and deep-seated feelings are aroused once someone initiates discussion on how we are admitting and educating our diverse students. Once the question is raised about how we are changing our curriculum, all armor is worn for the sake of protecting the venerable "quality" within our institutions.

In a recent discussion regarding the need for ethnic studies on our campus, a well-respected faculty member's first reaction toward the topic was that he would resist any effort to "ghetto-ize" the curriculum. This initial, and perhaps instinctive response, is that of protecting quality. The counterpoint perhaps ought to be that diversification of curriculum and ideas should be viewed as strongly aligned with quality rather than as a weakening of excellence. In truth, diversity is the balancing of quality and equity.

It is my contention that my experiences as a Chicano undergraduate are commonplace today in higher education. Entering minority students are all too often waging significant battles to survive their elementary and secondary experiences. As the cycle of American education reform has come and gone, many of our entering students still arrive with poor academic preparation, having fought the prejudices of society and our education systems. In other cases, such as Ricardo's, minority students may arrive with strong academic skills, however, accents, financial status, weak family support, and lack of broader educational experiences create greater challenges for succeeding in higher education.

How are our campuses organized to assist these students? In most cases, programs and services that assist minority students are still themselves peripheral and marginal in terms of the mission of the college or university. Has the core of the institution been modified in response to the changing student body? In the vast majority of instances, the response is no. There have been, in some instances, difficult dialogues; however, the core has not changed. In practice, what has occurred has been a half-hearted willingness to accept the challenges of increased minority students with token programs that insulate the core of the institution from any meaningful change. Minority-staffed programs and the few tenured minority faculty in our institutions have been the major impetus for assisting students from diverse backgrounds.

What we need to do during the 1990s and into the next century is to weave diversity into the full fabric of the institution, including the most fundamental relationship of all—the one between faculty and students.

There are a number of things that college professors can do to make their institution a better environment for diverse students. My suggestions are not based on analytical research, but rather on trial and error in coping within predominantly white institutions of higher learning. They are based on the basic human concepts of caring. If an organization or a singular professor wants to increase effectiveness with diverse students, then I would advise the following:

- acceptance of individuals
- visible behavior that denotes respect
- participation in meaningful dialogue about your goals
- creating a sense of community
- willingness to share and sacrifice for the sake of students—to be a mentor
- always express belief in students

As noted earlier, these are not original concepts. These were strategies that were used on my behalf, and I have continued to use them on my students' behalf. It is my belief that arguing for diversity will—on its own—not improve our institutions. What is called for is a personal and institutional conviction for diversity that will pay particular attention to the human issues of commonality, universality, unity, connectedness, belonging, and community.

Perhaps more poignant is the sincere realization that students from diverse backgrounds do belong at a university and that it is every faculty member's responsibility to teach every student effectively. The absolute starting point is that once you accept an individual, then you can move forward to effectively teach the student.

Acceptance of Individuals

The concept of equitable treatment of diverse cultures is not romanticized or unreasonable. What is unreasonable is the concept of one superior culture. In fact, a hierarchical analysis of cultures is highly questionable. As Ron Takaki (1993) writes in his recent book, *A Different Mirror*, not all persons were welcomed to the United States. Takaki illustrates the tremendous historical differences in treatment between racial and ethnic groups. As an example, he points out that most citizens know about Ellis Island as the entry point for most Europeans; however, very few know about Angel Island, the entry point for many Asians into the United States, and the negative associations many Asian Americans have with this particular island.

I clearly recall the time I was assigned the book titled *North From Mexico* by Carey McWilliams (1990), as a sophomore in college. It introduced me for the first time to a sociological review of the experience of Mexican Americans in the United States. The content of the book, although I may strongly argue different points of view now, presented me with a significant sense of validity and acceptance of my historical and present-day values. Studying my Mexican American identity, history, and sociopolitical role in America instilled a sense of belonging and legitimacy.

A similar experience can be achieved if faculty use their students' own sets of experiences. As an example, science majors can study how Chinese professors question the basic assumptions of Western medicine. How does Mexican folk medicine parallel, complement, and at times conflict with modern medicine? Political science majors should understand the role that Latin American university students play in their country's political spectrum. University students in Latin America not only study politics but have a significant role in shaping national political agendas.

Acceptance is in essence demonstrating a positive regard for students' pasts and cultural experiences. It is communicating a willingness to explore different realities other than one's own personal background. It means that faculty need to be willing to have students share their own insights, arguments, and experiences as part of the course content. It also means that faculty must be open to learning new concepts and perhaps even learning these new concepts from the very students they teach.

Behavior That Denotes Respect

Rhetoric that pronounces the "celebration of diversity" but is not followed up with specific behavior to demonstrate it is dysfunctional. What is called for are concrete forms of behavior that allow for differences of opinion yet foster interdependence. It is not simply creating tolerance of diversity, but rather full acceptance of divergent points of view. Perhaps the most sincere act of respect is the ability to express differences while not diminishing the other person. Faculty and administrators should not avoid conflict for the sake of keeping harmony. On the contrary, the development of mechanisms to identify and manage conflict is extremely useful.

Respect is not demonstrated by avoiding conflict; respect is absolute when community is still maintained despite disagreements. A campus should strive for an environment where differences are perceived as an enriching resource—one that yields a fuller understanding of individuals and society as a whole.

I have witnessed a fraternity singing songs about raping and killing women, a student group throwing tortillas and empty beer bottles at Hispanic students, and a professor who depicted African American males as drug dealers. These types of behaviors promote racist stereotypes. I look at these incidents as opportunities to discuss issues of diversity. To choose to ignore these behaviors is to assume they do not affect the learning environment and also communicates the hidden message that certain individuals are not valued or respected. Some examples of behaviors and strategies that denote respect are as follows:

• At the very basis of respect is the behavior of learning your students' names. As I say this, I acknowledge the great difficulty I have remembering individual names. It is not an easy task. Nonetheless, the impact of a having a professor remember one's name or a little extra caring in recalling where one is from is a gratifying and validating experience.

• Establish in your class a framework to assist students in feeling comfortable expressing divergent views. We as faculty must encourage discussion and debate; however, it must be within an environment that does not diminish the individual.

• Recall, if you will, instances when professors validated your arguments, discoveries, or input. Or recall when you were invited to the student union by your professor for a cup of coffee. The expression of caring for students as distinct individuals has a tremendous impact on students wanting and working toward excellence in the classroom.

• Critically important to this equation of respect is your ability to communicate your expectation for excellence by everyone. Expecting less from certain students is not equitable. The difficult task for faculty is developing strategies to assist students who need extra assistance. Assist students to achieve your expectations; do not lower your requirements.

• Participate in instructional improvement workshops for faculty that include methods for conducting discussions regarding diversity issues.

• If an incident occurs on campus that is clearly racist or sexist, direct and precise action must be used to address the situation. These kinds of incidents can provide opportunities to delineate appropriate and inappropriate behavior to the entire campus.

Dialogue Regarding Goals

The future vitality and viability of institutions of higher learning will require a fundamental examination and restatement of the social contract that links academe and society as a whole. The need to have the goals of institutions restated is based on two sets of functions that the university must perform. The first is a set of expectations that require scientific research to question all conclusions. Certainly no university nor faculty member will accept any research as unequivocal without thorough analysis and, if necessary, testing of all assumptions. Diversity of opinions and ideas is actually a cornerstone of intellectual inquiry. To many faculty, diversity of perspectives is tantamount to an ethical and moral imperative. Thus, given this scientific requirement to accept and even invite diversity of opinions, the mere questioning of the goals of an institution should be seen as a healthy and normal process.

The second set of concepts that ought to encourage a debate about goals is the social, economic, and educational contract with society. It is understood that for society to prosper, institutions of higher learning must be in step with the needs of citizens. If the university fails to understand or accept the new challenges or new diverse students into its mission, it risks losing its ability to deliver to society a core of educated citizens.

Universities must acknowledge that, like society, higher education is in the midst of transition. Faculty and institutions have found it extremely difficult to establish a climate of mutual respect and the mechanism that allows for discussion and change. Change for higher education and individual faculty has been extremely painful. Often, as noted earlier, creative innovation has been introduced by students or programs designed to help minority students. However, change that is introduced by anyone other than faculty is often greatly resisted. Most colleges and universities easily buy into the concept of diversity. In fact, it is stated that the "buy-in" is a social imperative; however, the change required to transform a university or college is met with much less enthusiasm.

It has been my observation that conflict among colleagues intensifies once explicit commitments are made toward diversity. The real question to colleagues is whether they truly want to honor the contract with society to educate all qualified citizens. It is a fact that campuses are becoming more diverse. Will campuses invite a debate regarding a mission that portrays the institution's willingness to cope with change? Will they address such issues as:

- Is the institution more concerned with assessing minority students for standards than improving program quality?
- Does the institution place more importance on numbers of diverse students than the quality of instruction provided to these students?
- Is the institution changing its programs to deal with diverse populations?
- Are faculty understanding and changing instructional strategies to conform to differences among students, or are they satisfied with the symbolic attempt to infuse issues and concepts with little or no effect on the core of the curriculum?
- Does the institution value differences of opinion?
- Is there effective communication between different groups on campus and administration and faculty?
- Do faculty value students who prefer to cooperate rather than compete?
- Do faculty members communicate to the class their preference to teach the "best and the brightest" students versus those students who need more encouragement and assistance?

Creating a Community

At most institutions, when one speaks about community in terms of minority students, most administrators will indicate the existence of student clubs; that is, the African American Student Alliance, the Chicano Student Association, MEChA, or the American Indian Club. Community for diverse students is often defined as each group having its own truth, its own organization. My particular concern with this relativistic perspective is that each of these singular approaches to community evolves toward separatism, not toward a cohesive community. This is not to suggest that minority student clubs are not positive; they are very important. In Chapter 7 of this book, Delores J. Huff effectively delineates the positive aspects of these types of student clubs. My remarks are directed at a broader university community of students. Minorities can often be active in minority student clubs and still feel isolated.

When I was at UCLA, the local university norm was for every student, ethnic, and special interest group to have its own student newspaper. These special interest groups would often advocate singularly for their own worthy cause. However, little was provided to assist students in exploring how they felt about each other. Furthermore, little was done to help students understand how these feelings enhanced or interfered with their social and educational goals. The effective campus community will be one that takes into account the whole community and not just the needs of the special interest groups. (For a more detailed discussion of campus community vis-à-vis communities of interest, see Book Six in this series, *Confronting Diversity Issues on Campus*, by Ben Bowser, Gale Auletta, and Terry Jones.)

Defining community can be accomplished by taking into consideration many items. A sense of community or the absence of one can be defined by many small events. Unfortunately, many campuses assume that community already exists or that it develops automatically; while other campuses think that students will take on the sense of community through some type of natural process. From my perspective, we cannot leave community-building to chance; nor can we ignore the need to provide orientation, training, mentoring, and the transmittal of values to our students. Attitudes about how individuals and groups belong are transmitted or exemplified through residential programs, campus-life activities, and interactions with faculty. In essence, how supportive and accepting an institution is toward individuals transmits a sense of belonging.

How students learn about their uniqueness and the expectation of achievement with a supportive environment is pivotal in sensing a level of belonging. For faculty to illustrate a sense of community, perhaps they can consider the following nonmonumental yet meaningful messages:

- Ask each student to share with you, and possibly with the class, what makes them unique as an individual.
- Make an extra effort to express appreciation when students participate in class discussions.
- Intervene immediately should a fellow student disparage a student's culture or language. Although this sounds easier said than done, the credibility of the faculty member is jeopardized if such occurrences are not dealt with at once. Society has encouraged and has been socialized to accept negative stereotypes. The media depict Hispanics and African Americans as criminals more than 80% of the time. Casual stereotyping in academic discussions should simply not occur.
- Encourage students to participate in university activities or community service. Common sense leads us to believe that individuals quickly feel a sense of belonging if they can invest in a group or contribute toward a project. Although most faculty are somewhat detached from university activities or student clubs, the value of those opportunities is tremendous for students. Becoming involved in minority student clubs or student government may be as valuable for a student as being invited to the department's bridge club or elected to the faculty senate is for faculty. The critical issue is to establish a sense of belonging to a community.
- Value the broad and varied sets of experiences that students bring to class not as liabilities but rather as potential resources. Can you as a professor inventory your students' exposure, interest, and strengths regarding the course content in order to incorporate their different learning styles and experiences into your teaching methods? Or do you teach the same content and use the same methods each term for every section?
- Demonstrate equitable treatment and expect excellence from all students. Equitable treatment would incorporate a variety of

assessment tools. As discussed in Chapters 5 and 6, assessment methods can truly have an effect on learning as well as communicating to students how you as an instructor value what they have learned.

Be a Mentor

Often, assisting students from diverse backgrounds requires more than what is normally expected of faculty and administrators. It is my personal experience that many individuals shared and sacrificed for me in order that I might succeed. Faculty and staff who went out of their way to assist were numerous. Their willingness to teach, mentor, share, and at times sacrifice their own needs portrayed to me an incredible investment and belief in my potential. It demonstrated a deep sense of caring.

Once an individual invests in your future, how easy is it to ignore those high expectations laid upon you? I shall never forget a professor in my master's program who instilled in me the belief that I should continue on toward my doctorate. The weight of Dr. Tomas Rivera saying to me, "Juan, you too, can be a Ph.D. si tienes las ganas (if you desire it)," was intoxicating. Taking the extra step in showing humanity and interdependence will go a long way in communicating a deep sense of acceptance. You will read a great deal more about mentoring in Delores Huff's Chapter 7. Here are the key messages I believe need to be shared in the mentoring relationship:

- Acknowledge that all college students feel vulnerable and out of place at times.
- Acknowledge that deciding what to be for the rest of their lives can be very intimidating.
- Understand that for some students the demands by family, culture, religion, and peers can make it very difficult to balance a traditional collegiate life.

- Acknowledge that part of being a student is having fun and learning to live a balanced life.
- Communicate that, yes, academic achievement is expected but not without a great deal of hard work.
- Share with your students your successes and failures in higher education. There are lessons to be learned from your experiences.
- Emphasize that your students' culture, language, and background are assets, not baggage to be left behind as they move through their college experience. Encourage their own self-identity.
- Entrust students with the responsibility of being caretakers for others. Sometimes you receive a great deal back when you give to others.

Express Belief in Students

The aforementioned concepts all rely on the inherent assumption that faculty and institutions actively believe that all students achieve. Although the role of chief executive officers and senior administrators is critically important in setting the tone for diversity on a campus, the central role of faculty is pertinent in communicating faith and belief in students. The active exchange between faculty and students dictates that the dialogue sets the principle tone for expectations.

This fundamental relationship between faculty and students suggests that the expressed belief that all students can achieve requires that diversity be woven into the core academic experience of students. This belief in educating all can be expressed through a curriculum that is reflective of the students being taught. My singular point of advice regarding this expression of belief is rather simple: *Express your belief in students in all of your interactions with them.*

To sum it up, once you accept, then you can teach.

References and Resources

Green, M. F. (Ed.). (1989). *Minorities on campus: A handbook for enhancing diversity.* Washington, DC: American Council on Education.

Lather, P. (1991). *Getting smart: Feminist research and pedagogy with/in the postmodern.* New York: Routledge.

McWilliams, C. (1990). *North from Mexico: The Spanish-speaking people of the United States* (updated by M. S. Meier). New York: Greenwood Press.

Omi, M., & Winant, H. (1986). *Racial formation in the United States: From 1960 to the 1980.* New York: Routledge.

Pascarella, E. T., & Terezini, P. T. (1991). *How college affects students.* San Francisco: Jossey-Bass.

Sleeter, C. (Ed.). (1991). *Empowerment through multicultural education.* New York: State University of New York Press.

Smith, D. G. (1989). The challenge of diversity: Implications for institutional research. In M. Nettles (Ed.), *New directions for institutional research: The effect of assessment on minority student participation, No. 65.* San Francisco: Jossey-Bass.

Takaki, R. (1993). *A different mirror: A history of multicultural America.* Boston: Little, Brown.

Varenne, H. (Ed.). (1986). *Symbolizing America.* Lincoln, Nebraska: University of Nebraska Press.

Wong, F. (1991). Diversity and community: Right objectives and wrong arguments. *Change: The Magazine of Higher Learning, 23*(4), 48-54.

2 | Diversity and Change on Campus

HELEN ROBERTS

Twenty years ago, while doing research for my doctoral thesis on multicultural curriculum, I studied the forces in our society that were compelling elementary and secondary schools to change; forces such as the renewed aspirations of families for their children following the civil rights breakthroughs of the 1960s and the large immigration of refugees following the Southeast Asian War. I had chosen for my thesis the problem of "A Design for Developing Multicultural Curriculum." At that time, it was a very esoteric topic. Multicultural education was considered to be a concern only of K-12 education, and really only for urban schools.

Today, the K-12 educational issues of the 1970s have grown up and gone to college. Last year's demographic predictions have become this year's headlines in the *Chronicle of Higher Education*, headlines like:

Educators Must Resolve Multicultural Conflicts
Has Race Become an Admissions Issue?
Regional Accrediting Agencies Prod Colleges on Diversity
Rethinking the Culture of Disciplines

Colleges Must Recognize Students' Cognitive Styles
We Must Deal With Foreign Students' Language Problems

These stories are evidence of the changes that have occurred in America's colleges and universities; changes that began with a changing student population but have had a broad impact on every aspect of campus life, from the canon of the disciplines to academic freedom itself.

Getting Reaquainted With Ourselves

How has diversity changed your campus over the years? If you haven't taken a hard look recently, you should. A good place to begin would be at the office that keeps track of your campus characteristics. It might be the institutional research office, or perhaps the registrar. To get an overall picture of changes on your campus, I suggest that you compare differences over the past 10 or 15 years. Pick two years for which you can get good data and complete the chart in Table 2.1.

Take some time to talk with colleagues about the implications of what you have learned. If your campus is like most others in this country, it is probably more diverse now than it was then. And even if your student profile has remained relatively stable, it is important to recognize that the business world for your graduates is an international, multicultural climate in which intergroup skills are essential. You might want to compare your campus with other campuses, or with the national trends described in the next section, and project the trends for your own institution in the future.

In taking stock of diversity on your campus, you should also familiarize yourself with institutional policies and procedures, specialized recruitment and retention programs, academic programs, instructional support, and administrative offices that might be available to assist you and your students. Have these policies and programs kept pace with the changing student population? A very helpful guide for assessing campus diver-

Table 2.1 Diversity and Change on Campus

	Department		Campus	
	Then	*Now*	*Then*	*Now*
Number of students:				
Full-time				
Part-time				
Age distribution of students:				
16-21				
22-34				
35 or older				
Percentage of students who are:				
African American				
American Indian/Native American				
Asian American/Pacific Islander				
Hispanic or Latino				
White/Anglo American				
Women				
Men				
Foreign students				
Foreign born/recent immigrants				
Living in campus residence halls				
Working 20 hours/week				
Working 40 hours/week				
Receiving financial aid				
Percentage of faculty who are:				
African American				
American Indian/Native American				
Asian American/Pacific Islander				
Hispanic or Latino				
White/Anglo American				
Women				
Men				
Foreign students				
Foreign born/recent immigrants				

sity is Madeleine F. Greene's (1989) *Minorities on Campus: A Handbook for Enhancing Diversity,* published by the American Council on Education. It is chock full of ideas and strategies and sample programs for improving the campus climate for diverse students.

The Myth of the "Typical" College Student

If there ever was a "typical" college student, there isn't one these days. Students in higher education institutions across the country are becoming more and more diverse. If the "traditional" or typical college student used to be white, middle class, and fresh out of high school, then by marked contrast, today's college students are:

Older. Only about half of U.S. college students are in the 16-21 age group today. In fact, nearly 15% of all college students are more than 35 years of age.

More ethnic minorities. One in every five college students today is from a racial or ethnic minority group. Between 1980 and 1990 enrollment of Hispanic Americans increased by 66%, African American enrollments were up 13%, Asian American/ Pacific Islander enrollments were up 100%, and American Indian enrollments increased by 23%. (Overall enrollments in higher education increased by 18% in the same time period.)

More women than men. Women now make up 55% of all students enrolled in college, although they are still disproportionately underrepresented in certain major academic fields, especially the sciences, as are ethnic minority students.

More often foreign born, with English as a second language. Recent immigration, particularly from Latin America and Asia, means that more foreign born students than ever are entering American higher education. Although there are no national statistics available on these students, California has estimated that 33% of its public school children come from families where English is not the primary language spoken at home.

More likely to be a part-time student. Nearly half of all college students are part-time students. Today's students are also much more likely to have significant family responsibilities, including childrearing, and other community obligations beyond campus life.

More likely to need financial assistance. Whereas college costs have continued to rise, financial aid has not kept pace. In fact, when measured in constant dollars, the average federal student aid grant or loan is worth less today than it was 10 years ago. Students are not getting as much help from their parents as they used to, either. A recent study in California showed that 42% of all full-time college students are financially independent of their parents, and 78% of part-time students are supporting themselves.

Working more hours on jobs unrelated to their coursework. The lack of adequate financial aid, coupled with the increasing age of students, means that more students are working longer hours. Again, there are no national statistics collected on this, but one survey by the California Student Aid Commission found that 70% of California's full-time students are working. For full-time undergraduate students in four-year colleges, 31% work more than 20 hours per week; and more than 41% of all part-time undergraduates work 40 or more hours per week.

When you think about the significant implications of these trends, its no wonder that our traditional college curriculum and instructional methods are not working as well as they used to. The wide diversity of experience that students bring with them to the classroom, coupled with the significant responsibilities they have outside of their college program, present enormous challenges to faculty in teaching and advising their students.

Access and Success

Although our colleges and universities can be very proud of the rapid increases in the number of minority students enrolled in recent years, there are still two critical problems we have to face.

First, the increasing minority population of the United States is far outstripping the participation of these groups in higher education. For example, in 1990, Hispanics made up about 9% of the population of the United States, and 8.3% of high school graduates, but only 5.6% of the college students. African American, American Indian, and many Asian American groups show similarly low "college-going rates." That's the access problem, and we haven't solved it yet.

Second, for those minority students who do go to college, their persistence and degree completion rates are not comparable to the rates for white students. According to the National Center for Education Statistics Survey *High School and Beyond*, it is estimated that for students who began college in 1980 as full time freshmen, after $5\frac{1}{2}$ years, 55.8% of white students had attained the bachelors degree, compared with 49.8% of Asian Americans, 32.3% of Latino students, and only 30.3% of African American students. The higher college dropout rates and the longer "time-to-degree" are causing minority populations to lag farther and farther behind in their higher education completion.

What can faculty do to turn these problems around and improve both access and success for all students? It starts with getting to know the students a whole lot better, setting high expectations for achievement, and then taking from the proven educational methods those ones that promote the most intense engagement of students and faculty together with the subject matter.

Setting the Stage for Success in Your Department

The remaining chapters of this book are devoted to what you can do to enhance students' classroom success by using multicultural approaches in your teaching. Here, I'm going to mention five things your department can do to set the stage for success of diverse students in your major.

❶ **Find out more about your students.** How much do you know about the students in your department? Does your department regularly collect (and do the faculty regularly discuss) information about the circumstances of your students' lives that affect their education? The Appendix of this book contains a good example of a departmental student survey. Developed by Carol Barnett, chair of the Biology Department at San Diego State University, it covers demographic and cultural backgrounds, pathways to the university, motivations and goals, financial status, living and working conditions, curricular progress and problems, and study habits. She used the results of this survey to develop a profile of students majoring in biology, microbiology, and environmental health and to stimulate faculty discussion about changes in curricular and student support programs.

If your department doesn't have a survey like this, I suggest you start one. You may also want to begin surveying your alumni to get advice and feedback on how well your major prepared them for their career and their civic responsibilities.

❷ Next, review the curriculum from the perspective of diversity and change. Examine your department's contribution to your institution's general educational program as well as to your major field. Does your curriculum reflect the latest thinking on multicultural perspectives in your field? Does it introduce students to the contributions of scholars from different cultural backgrounds and perspectives? Have your departmental goals been reviewed in the light of diversity and change on your campus?

If you are undertaking such a review, you are in good company. As of 1992, one third of U.S. colleges reported they require specific coursework that focuses on multicultural issues, and another 15% say that multicultural requirements are under consideration. Multicultural approaches are also critical in the preparation of teachers— a major responsibility of higher education institutions. Thirty-seven states now require candidates for teacher certification to have coursework and/or fieldwork on the role of culture in how children learn, and ten states require that the student teaching experience be in a multicultural setting. Does your departmental curriculum help your institution to meet these standards? Chapter 4 by Otis Scott has a wealth of curriculum/content revision strategies and resources to help you get started.

❸ Tie assessments of student progress to academic advising. The third thing your department can do is review its advising program to make sure that students of all backgrounds are getting the benefit of good academic advising. This should include direct feedback to the students regarding their progress in the major and the opportunities that are available to them as they proceed through their course of studies. And remember, issuing departmental reminders about deadlines for requirements isn't enough. An ongoing personal relationship should be established with each student, and information should be shared on a regular basis so that there are no surprises. You want to be the first to know if a student starts to experience trouble, rather than the last.

❹ **Encourage promising minority students to consider academic careers.** Who will carry the torch when you retire? Where will the next generation of faculty in your discipline come from? We know that faculty diversity has not kept up with student diversity, because nearly 90% of all full-time faculty are white. By the year 2000, one third of all Americans will be ethnic or racial minorities, and most new jobs will require some level of postsecondary education. This means we simply haven't gotten enough minority students through graduate programs and into faculty positions.

You and your department can increase the number of underrepresented students who will succeed in graduate studies in your discipline by doing a few simple things:

- Identify promising undergraduate students early.
- Establish meaningful personal relationships between these students and faculty within the department.
- Provide opportunities for students to teach in your discipline through tutoring or teaching assistantships.
- Provide opportunities for students to engage in research studies along with faculty.
- Identify problems students are encountering and devise support systems to help them overcome the problems.

For more ideas and techniques on advising and mentoring, turn to Chapter 1 by Juan C. Gonzales and Chapter 7 by Delores J. Huff.

❺ **Expand your department's outreach to K-12 schools.** I don't know of a college or a department that is not concerned about the preparation that their students have received. As K-12 school budgets have been stretched to the breaking point, more and more students are missing some of the important prerequisites for college-level work.

By expanding your department's outreach to K-12 schools, you can both improve the college preparedness of students and recruit more diverse students to major in your field. Here are some low-cost things you can do to expand your outreach:

- Start a local "Academic Alliance" for K-12 and college faculty in your discipline; sponsor colloquia and seminars on topics of mutual interest in your discipline.
- Establish electronic mail connections between your department and the teachers in the schools; use each other's expertise in addressing teaching and learning issues.
- Organize a student-to-student mentoring and/or tutoring program for students in your major to work in local schools.
- Jointly review curriculum and assessments, placement, and admissions issues that affect the smooth transition of students from school to college.

You Are Not Alone:
Developing a List of Campus Resources

There are lots of resources to help you in developing multicultural approaches on your campus. If no one has compiled a listing for your campus, you might want to do that and share it with other departments. Be sure to include:

- ethnic, minority, international, foreign language, and other student or faculty clubs or service organizations
- counseling and advising programs
- programs to enhance student diversity in the major fields
- student mentoring, tutoring, and support programs
- learning assistance programs
- special orientation or summer bridge programs
- outreach to students in K-12 schools
- special collections in the library

- faculty expertise related to multicultural diversity
- faculty professional development, instructional development, or curriculum development programs

In addition, there are a number of federal, state, and private programs that provide funding for the above. There are some especially good federally funded opportunities in the sciences and technical fields, such as the National Science Foundation's Alliances for Minority Participation program (AMP), the National Institutes for Health's Minority Biomedical Research Support program (MBRS), or the interagency Minority Access to Research Careers program (MARC). California and several other states also encourage underrepresented students to enter mathematics-based careers through such programs as MESA (Mathematics, Engineering, Science Achievement) and MEP (the MESA Engineering Program). Enlist the help of your campus grants and research office in finding support for the initiatives you want to undertake.

Most of all, remember that you are not alone! The better you know and use your campus' resources, the better equipped you will be to help students to achieve and the easier it will be to work with your faculty colleagues to create the positive learning climate that all of our students deserve.

References and Resources

California Student Aid Commission. (1993). *The California undergraduate: A financial and demographic profile.* Sacramento: Author.

Carter, D. J., & Wilson, R. (1992). *Eleventh annual status report on minorities in higher education.* Washington, DC: American Council on Education, Office of Minorities in Higher Education.

Education Commission of the States, National Task Force on Minority Achievement in Higher Education. (1990). *Achieving campus diversity: Policies for change.* Denver, CO: Author.

Green, M. F. (Ed.). (1989). *Minorities on campus: A handbook for enhancing diversity.* Washington, DC: American Council on Education.

Intersegmental Coordinating Council, Curriculum and Assessment Cluster Committee. (1989). *California's limited English language students: An intersegmental agenda.* Sacramento: Author.

U.S. Department of Education, National Center for Education Statistics. (1992a). *The condition of education, 1992.* Washington, DC: Author.

U.S. Department of Education, National Center for Education Statistics. (1992b). *Digest of education statistics, 1992.* Washington, DC: Author.

U.S. Department of Education, National Center for Education Statistics. *High School and Beyond.* Database maintained by NCES, Washington, DC.

U.S. Department of Education, National Center for Education Statistics. (1993). *Trends in enrollment in higher education by racial/ethnic category: Fall 1980 through Fall 1991.* Washington, DC: Author.

3 | Teaching All Students Equally

RAY LOU

Grappling with the issues of teaching students from different races, ethnicities, cultures, economic strata, and life stages has been one of my preoccupations since I first stepped into a classroom as an instructor. That first experience was a real eye-opener. I quickly discovered that I could not teach this class of low-income students, mostly people of color, by simply imitating the styles of my favorite professors. The stand-behind-the-lectern and hold-their-attention-with-strategic-interjections-of-sarcastic-humor method of lecturing failed miserably. I was miserable. The students who stayed were miserable. Most students were bright enough not to prolong their suffering and dropped out of the class. I was left behind the lectern lecturing to an almost empty classroom and wondering how I could improve the students' learning experience.

At the time, the middle 1970s, I thought that my failure was due to my inexperience. After all, I was but a naive graduate student. So I consulted with my advisers and favorite professors on what I was doing wrong. I even asked two of them to come and observe my teaching. I found their responses reassuring. According to them, the failure was not mine as a lecturer; after all, they were the models of teaching excellence that I followed. Rather, the failure to learn was the fault of the students.

The students in my class were not "regular" students. Aside from being mostly low-income students of color, the class was filled with "special admits," students who did not meet the customary academic admissions standards of the institution and were admitted after special consideration. These students were part of the university's affirmative action plan to increase the numbers of nonwhite students on campus.

My professors' advice on how to improve the students' learning was to change the students. Although they may have secretly wanted to do this, they did not recommend exchanging this group for another group of better prepared, higher achieving students, but to remake these students in the mold of regular students. I, as the instructor, was told not to change either the content or the methods of my teaching. To do so, I was instructed, was to lower academic standards.

My professors told me that the institution's responsibility as the standard-bearer for society was not to be taken lightly. They told me that it was obligatory for the students to meet the standards of the institution. I was assured that this was not simply a sink or swim proposition. The institution also took its responsibility to these special students seriously. It established programs in academic survival for these students in an effort to remake them into successful ones. Everything from note taking to time management to use of the library was covered.

I was told that my role in assisting the students' adjustment to the university was to be a model of traditional academic excellence. After all, what better role model could the students have? I, a person of color from a peasant family, had made the necessary personal accommodation to be successful in the academy without the assistance of the special programs that were created for these students. All these students had to do to make it through the university was to be disciplined and change their work ethic. I was assured that my primary value to these students was to behave in the manner of my professors:

go to class, lecture, hold office hours, and act professorial. If students had problems with the lecture material that I could not clarify in a brief period of time, I was to refer them to my teaching assistant or to the staff of the academic survival programs, which, according to my professors, bore the responsibility for academic success of these students.

The undergirding principle of these programs is that the student is deficient and must be brought up to the institution's standards to facilitate his or her progress. Understood but unstated in this rationale was the notion that current methods of delivering instruction to college students should not be modified. This sequence followed closely the traditional race relations theory developed by sociologist Robert Park in the 1920s. To wit: a small minority population would be assimilated into mainstream society after a period of accommodation or adjustment by the newcomers. On college campuses, it was expected that the accommodation process that these new students would go through would be made easier by the operation of academic survival programs.

As I learned from my experience as a college instructor, the real world success of this model, like the race relations theory it was built upon, was limited. No matter how prepared or motivated students were or how many survival skills classes they attended, I found that in order to improve their learning, I had to change my teaching methods to meet their needs. Sure, the academic survival courses helped. And for some students, they made a significant difference in their academic performance, regardless of their income or skin color. But in order to engage the student, to see the lightbulbs turn on and glow, to see them excel, I had to do more than lace my lectures with sardonic witticisms.

This was a hard lesson for me to swallow. It was a popular belief that the reason so many students of color failed in college was due to their lack of preparation or motivation or lack of family reinforcement for the tradition of higher education. Believing in these explanations myself, I became very active in the campus academic survival programs. I counseled students.

I met with them out of class. I socialized with them. I tutored them in subjects that I had some knowledge of. I met their families and talked to them about their students' progress. I made sure they were prepared for class. I did practically everything but attend their classes and take their exams. But the end result was not much better than before I became involved.

I knew something was wrong, but not what. I knew the students were not dumb. Many of them had exceptional abilities. I knew the students were highly motivated to succeed. They and their families knew that they were being given an opportunity that was uncommon for people from their backgrounds. Family support for these kids was intense. They wanted these students to succeed. Most students felt a strong obligation to succeed for their families. I made sure that the kids I worked with studied and were well-prepared for class. But their performance remained mediocre.

The exception to this was a small number of students in this group who were enrolled in a class that I was teaching. Their performance in my class was outstanding. In other classes, they did about as well as the remainder of the group. My first reaction to this difference was to dismiss it because of my close association with these individuals. They received special treatment. I met with them after class. They hung around my office. We were friends. Invariably during our conversations, I would point out how things in their personal lives or in current events illustrated elements from our course material. Often in class I would call on them to answer questions. Moreover, I would call them by name, something I did not do with other students because I did not know them. But I tried to be objective in my judgment of their work and how I treated them in class. I called on these students often, not because I knew them but because they were the best students in the class. They simply knew the subject far better than their classmates.

It took me many years of separation from this group of students to realize the significance of my observations of their academic performance. Only after numerous modifications of my teaching style and countless classroom experiments did I come to accept the lesson taught by the students I worked with in the academic survival program: the failure of nontraditional students was not their fault. The failure of low-income students of color to excel in all areas of the academy was not due to their inadequacies as students but the inability of the institution to address their learning needs.

This point is driven home by recent research on the academic performance of minority students in math-based subjects by science educator Uri Treisman. In brief, minority students participating in Treisman workshops in mathematics and science courses performed at significantly higher levels compared to their classmates who did not attend the workshops. His model has been duplicated at numerous campuses, both two- and four-year colleges, with similar results. What Treisman and his many followers are able to demonstrate in convincing fashion is that it is not the students who are deficient, it is the mode of instruction (see, for example, Treisman, 1992; Treisman & Fullilove, 1990; Treisman & Garland, 1993).

What follows is a discussion of my general principles for teaching students from diverse backgrounds. These principles and their applications have evolved from my own stumbling trial-and-error experiments in classes filled with diverse students. My principles for good teaching in a multicultural classroom do not displace the "Seven Principles for Good Practice in Undergraduate Education," set forth by Arthur Chickering and Zelda Gamson in their wildly popular article published in 1987. Rather than displace, they supplement by applying accepted principles of good teaching to the particular learning needs of diverse students. The question that I have had to wrestle with over the years of teaching students of color and other students "from the margins of our society" is, "Are the principles for good teaching different for minority students and Euramericans?" Early on in my career I thought the answer was certainly yes. Minority students have different and varying learning styles, cultures, worldviews, and self-images. To teach these students effectively, one had to employ appropriate methods of instruction. But after becoming more familiar with current research in teaching and learning, I realized that in becoming a better teacher of minority students, I had become a better teacher of white students. In other words, I have not developed a competing set of good teaching principles for minority students and another for white students: principles for good teaching apply to all students. It is the application and context of these principles that must be varied to match the learning needs of diverse students.

I have developed a context for applying good teaching principles to classrooms of diverse student learners. I have but one specific principle for teachers of diverse students: teach all students equally. There are three prerequisites that educators must satisfy before they can teach all students equally.

Three Prerequisites to Teaching All Students Equally: Attitude, Perspective, and Knowledge

The first prerequisite to becoming a better practitioner in a multicultural classroom is having the attitudinal openness to improving your classroom practices. Although this may seem like a commonsensical starting place, it is important we realize that this attitude is the beginning point of our reconceptualization of what it means to be a college professor. For I contend that we, as professors, must also be students of our students in our own classrooms. This means that in order to be effective in a classroom of diverse students, we must reject the traditional model of college teaching—that the student must conform to the norms of the professor. Simply put, you cannot expect your students to clone your preferred way of learning.

The second prerequisite is to have an understanding of our own cultural perspectives. In order to address the needs of diverse students, we need to realize that we, even though we are members of the professoriate, are also active participants in the present mosaic of campus diversity. That although we may be different from most of our students—no matter what your perspective, professors are a pretty odd group—we have no greater claim to cultural legitimacy than any of our students. Please note that I do not question your classroom position of authority in your field of expertise. To say that your cultural perspective is no more legitimate than your students' is not to undermine your role as professor; nor is it to assert that your students possess equal knowledge. My point here is that when we enter the classroom we, too, bring with us perspectives and biases, as our students do, that may interfere with our ability to teach all students equally.

Although many of us go to great lengths to be consistent with all students in our classroom practices, this does not necessarily mean that we are neutral in our interaction with all students. In spite of our best intentions to the contrary, without systematically examining how we interact with people different from ourselves, we may never realize our differential behavior. Differential reaction to diverse students can negatively affect students' learning. Hence, it is necessary for us to take stock of our cultural baggage and assess how this may affect our teaching of diverse students.

Third, we must be knowledgeable about our students' different modes of learning. In general, as professional classroom practitioners, we must have a basic understanding of conceptual models of culture, its components, and the process of culture change. In particular, we must have a working knowledge of our students' cultural experiences, and how these experiences have shaped their modes of learning. Because we are all products of hierarchical societies, this knowledge must be informed by a basic understanding of the dynamics of racism, sexism, and other forms of structured inequality. I do not assert this because of some unconscious desire to make all college professors sociologists or flag-bearers for whatever cause, for the truth of the matter is that so many of our students come from backgrounds that were, until very recently and in many cases still are, considered marginal and illegitimate. If we are to teach diverse students equally well, we must understand how the contours of their self-identities may influence their classroom interactions with classmates different from themselves as well as us. We must understand that many students in our classroom come from groups who were excluded from fully participating in our society. We must understand how their backgrounds will affect their relationship with us and their classmates. This understanding is critical to our efforts to improve our teaching.

Teaching All Students Equally

Whereas the three prerequisites are the foundation upon which you will develop, the key principle to teaching effectively to diverse students, including students of color and others from the margins of our society, is to teach all students equally. Although I alluded to this in the previous section, it is important to note that this principle is fundamentally different conceptually and practically from the practice of being consistent with all students. A professor's consistent style of teaching may be unconsciously and consistently biased against a group of students in the class. The most available example of this is the research on gender bias in the classroom. Studies of classroom dynamics demonstrate that teachers are far more likely to interact with white male students. Women and men of color are less likely to be called upon and receive less attention from instructors in the college classroom.

Another example of unconscious differential treatment is how many of us react when communicating with a non-native speaker of English. When listening to a question or response from an ESL student, our faces often take on the pained expression of intense concentration complete with furrowed brows. Although we may have assumed this posture for the best of reasons, to listen carefully, we discourage their future participation in classroom discussions.

An example of how unconscious differential treatment of students from different backgrounds not only impedes the learning process but injures the self-image of these students comes from talking with students about the quality of their campus experiences. Sometimes when walking across the campus, I join a group of students to inquire about problems they face on campus. On this day I happened to encounter a group of Asian American students who expressed insult and hurt that their professor seldom called on them to participate in class discussions or to answer questions. What particularly upset them was that this professor seemed to have taken the time and effort to learn the names of Euramerican students and called on them by name. The professor never called on Asian American students by name but simply gestured or pointed in their direction if they raised their hands for recognition. Moreover, the group felt that when the ESL students among them spoke, the professor was curt and impatient. The dilemma for the students was that class participation was a factor in determining the class grade. Although the students were hurt by their exclusion from participation, they felt humiliated when they spoke. The students were convinced the professor was a racist. Fearing retaliation by the professor, they asked me not to intervene. They were simply thankful that an official of the university took the time to solicit their feelings about campus life.

Honoring the students' request, I did not intervene. But I knew the professor. I was anxious to confer with him about the students' perceptions. I knew him to be an ethical, conscientious classroom practitioner who cared about his students. In fact, I thought of him as one of the campus's better teachers. I also knew he was not a racist and he tried to treat students as fairly as possible. It was the next term, when we were leaving a committee meeting together, that I brought up the subject and summarized the students' complaints. He was crushed by these observations. He had no idea his discomfort in pronouncing Asian names could produce such negative results. He thought he had compensated for his shortcoming by recognizing Asian students with friendly gestures and eye contact. He was not conscious of excluding Asian students from class participation. He saw his classroom practice as equitable and impartial.

In order to minimize unconscious negative classroom practices of this nature, we must expand our repertoire of requisite classroom skills. Not only must we have a basic understanding of our students' different learning styles, we must develop the necessary skills to address each group present in the class. Based on my experience working with students of various stages and styles of learning, here is a condensed list of requisite skills for the teacher of diverse students.

❶ **Be a classroom activist.** You should be ready and able to take on different roles for different students and to vary your methods of instruction to ensure that you address all students. At times it may be appropriate for you be a coach, cheerleader, or promoter of students. Other students may learn best from a mentor or guide. Still others may need to relate to a taskmaster or authoritarian figure. You should develop the skill with which to discern students' educational needs and adjust your response accordingly.

❷ **Be comfortable facilitating active classroom learning.** Some students have their best learning experiences in small groups where the teaching is shared mutually by all participants. You should develop the skills to structure peer learning exercises. The structure of groups should promote a wide cross-section of student interaction. You must be active in monitoring and facilitating the group process. Left to its own, the group process may go awry. Other students may be driven to distraction by group learning. Some of these students learn better by engaging in simulation exercises or supervised fieldwork. You should develop exercises that incorporate multiple forms of learning: concrete as well as abstract; relational as well as analytical; reflective as well as observational; competitive as well as collaborative. It is important that you develop the ability to take your cues from your students in planning and scheduling appropriate class assignments.

❸ **Incorporate new scholarship about minorities, women, and other previously excluded groups into routine course materials.** Such information should be an integral part of your curriculum rather than an added-on or special feature such as "women's day" or "the minority lecture" introduced as required materials that you have no interest or expertise in. As a matter of perspective, you should view new scholarship and conceptual breakthroughs as enhancements for your classroom experience rather than as paradigmatic challenges that threaten your standing as a scholar. Students, particularly those from the margins of our society, are sensitive to your attitudes and can easily distinguish between a sincere attempt to be inclusive and one done with disdain, however dissembled.

❹ **Create and maintain a safe and supportive learning environment for all students in your classroom.** It is one thing to encourage students to be respectful of each other. It is another thing to create and preserve an environment in which every student feels comfortable with his or her perspectives and biases and knows how to express them without offending others. In order to do this, you must have the requisite skill, knowledge, and sensitivity to intervene appropriately when students consciously or unconsciously denigrate others in the class. You must be active in creating this environment. You cannot assume that students come to class with these skills. This environment must be cultivated and nurtured. It will not develop on its own. You must also equip students with the appropriate communication skills to intervene for themselves in a safe manner in the event you are not aware of violations to the environment for safe learning. This is especially important when your class is predominantly white and you are deficient in your understanding of the dynamics of racism. The same principle applies for classrooms with any gross imbalances between mainstream and minority students. Students from the margins of society must see themselves as legitimate and valued members of your class. They must be supported by you in their efforts to voice their perspectives without being made to think they are deviants.

❺ **Establish a program that will permit you to continuously assess student learning in your classroom.** Aside from the openness to take necessary action to improve your teaching methods, perhaps this is the most crucial ingredient in addressing the issues of diversity in your classroom. For without monitoring what your students' learning needs are, how will you know which facet of your teaching skills you need to improve? Guidelines and suggestions for establishing your own classroom assessment program appear later in this chapter and also in more detail in Chapters 5 and 6.

❻ **Practice these skills every day.** This sixth item on my list of requisite skills for the competent classroom practitioner for diverse students is not so much a skill as a commitment. In order to become expert at addressing the classroom needs of a multicultural student body you should develop and follow a regimen that will allow you to practice each of the five skills until they become an unconscious part of your daily routine.

Even though you may become quite adept at reading students and determining their learning needs, it is important that you use various methods and play different roles and keep rotating them to ensure that you address all the learning styles in your class. The fact that not all students respond equally to all styles of teaching makes a variety of methods highly desirable. The fact that some of these methods may conflict with students' learning makes variety and rotation mandatory.

An example of how a teaching method may conflict with and actually hinder student learning is the use of group learning exercises. Group exercises—discussion in small groups, group projects, problem solving breakout groups—are an important aspect of active learning, one of the Seven Principles for good teaching that everyone agrees should guide our teaching practices. However, when and how you implement group activities in your class are important factors to consider. Most experts agree that interactive learning among students should be promoted in structured situations with assigned shared or mutual learning tasks. But if these exercises are done in class, some students, particularly first-generation Asian Americans and other students from cultures who view the educational process as hierarchical, may passively resist. These students tend to view active participation as inappropriate classroom behavior because they regard the professor as the absolute authority and are not comfortable in engaging him or her in debate. As for group exercises in the classroom, students have occasionally said that student participation was a way for the professor to shirk teaching responsibilities. These students have difficulty seeing that student participation is another method of classroom learning. They feel cheated by the professor. In-class student interaction exercises are unimportant "play" rather than "real" learning. They felt that they were wasting valuable classroom time. These students felt that the only way teaching and learning was to be done was for the professor to tell them what they should know.

These students may feel threatened by the act of becoming engaged in their learning process. Interactive learning requires more effort from them; they no longer have the luxury of sitting passively. They are called upon to be responsible agents in determining their level of understanding the course material. Seen from this perspective, the students who remarked that student participation was a way for me to avoid my responsibilities for teaching the class were partially correct—rather than shoulder the total responsibility for student learning, I require my students to share this responsibility. Once I explain this and tell the students why I employ different methods of teaching and learning, the level of resistance usually diminishes.

However, some students, particularly ESL speakers, may be literally terrified by the thought of speaking out in class, even in a small-group setting. In classes where ESL students are present, I usually facilitate the small-group development process by having them start by sharing written assignments. If I sense terror and great reluctance to speak out, I try to address their fears by talking to the whole class about how important everyone's participation is to the class learning experience. I talk about how the act of communicating with each other in our multicultural society requires the development of better listening skills to become more literate in the speaking styles of others. Whether this eases their anxiety is questionable. It is only after students are walked through a couple of structured group exercises and discuss their learning process in those exercises that some become enthusiastic participants. By the end of the term, the level of communicative literacy of the entire class develops to a point where ESL students are no longer self-conscious about participating.

At this time the pertinent question is, "How do I acquire these requisite skills without overwhelming myself and neglecting my other professional duties?" My answer is that you should view your development as an expert teacher of diverse students as a continuous and never-ending process. A personal goal should be to continually improve your classroom skills for as long as you are a college professor. I don't think it is possible to reach a state of perfection in our profession. The frontiers of classrooms are constantly changing, and we must refine our teaching techniques to remain effective. In expanding your repertoire of classroom skills, it is important to set realistic goals for yourself with the knowledge that this is indeed a long-term plan. One way to approach this is to commit to a plan to add one new classroom skill to your personal repertoire each term. For example, you may decide to become conversant with one new learning style and its appropriate teaching style each term. The important thing is for you to maintain the readiness to expand your repertoire of skills. What you will probably discover is that this process will motivate you to expand your education farther than you anticipated. A little knowledge can be quite infectious.

This is but one approach. It is an approach that is relatively arbitrary. It is up to the individual professor to decide what aspect of her or his teaching to improve. Eventually, the professor will develop skills in all five areas. But how does the professor know which skill to develop first in order to meet the most pressing student need? In order to determine what teaching skill should be developed before others, a more systematic approach is called for.

Customer Satisfaction:
A Systematic and Incremental Approach

A systematic approach to the development of teaching skills calls for an inventory and assessment of your current repertoire. You may need to enlist the aid of some of your colleagues in completing this task. Certainly you will need the aid of your students. You should determine what are your strong and weak points as a teacher. Given this teaching profile, how well do you meet the learning needs of your students? How close do you come to teaching all students equally well? In addition to this process of self-evaluation, the answers to these questions lie in your continuous program of student outcomes assessment.

There are various methods of measuring student learning outcomes. Although certainly not the most reliable form of feedback, our own examinations and assignments provide us with some indication of what students are learning and how well. A useful exercise is to analyze student performance by the types of questions, examination formats, or assignments to determine if performance patterns are evident. Information gained from this analysis can help us improve the kinds of questions we ask students as well as the format. This kind of analysis can also indicate content areas that might need more emphasis. However, analyzing student performance data from class tests and assignments without having established previous controls offers little insight as to how we might improve the methods of instruction.

A comprehensive method of gauging student learning is to have an outside evaluator assess our students. Although this method offers valuable information about the overall intellectual growth of our students, it does not provide much insight into how we might improve our daily routine of classroom interaction. Moreover, this method is impractical to implement in each of our courses every term.

It is more realistic for us to augment the insight gained from our analyses of classroom tests and assignments with information solicited directly from the students. Although I used the term "outcomes assessment" as a descriptor for obtaining information about the learning needs of our students, a better term might be "customer satisfaction" surveys. What I am getting at here is that as instructors in the classroom, we need immediate comments from our students about the effectiveness of our teaching methods. Most outcomes assessment procedures offer only indirect information about our teaching styles. They may tell us what students learned but not why they learned or what we did to facilitate that learning.

In order to get this information, we have to ask our students directly. You may use a survey questionnaire, but I find asking students open-ended questions like "What suggestions do you have for me in covering Topic X that would make the subject more interesting or of value to you?" more useful in gaining information that allows me to alter my teaching. You may ask students to respond to these questions in writing. In this case, I structure the response by providing them with a limited amount of time, say three minutes, or a number of written lines. At other times, I use some version of the one- or five-minute writing exercise. I usually ask the class to write for five minutes on the most important thing they learned this class period. More often, I simply hold periodic open classroom discussions to assess my teaching. I set the stage for these discussions by telling the class at the beginning of the term about my goal for improving their classroom learning experience. Students' response to this method has been very instructive for me.

This format works well in small to medium-size classes. In larger lecture sections, open discussions are problematic. Only the most assertive students will be heard. You may ask for written responses in these classes, although I find this format less helpful. A technique I have used with some success is forming a representative "quality control team" of students who meet with me on a weekly basis to discuss the quality of instruction. The critique offered by these groups can be most useful to you. Not only do you receive comments about the mundane mechanics of your teaching like, "You need to use more pressure when you write on the chalkboard to make darker marks so students in the back of the room don't have to strain their eyes to decipher your writing" or "You pace too much," you also gain a sense of how well they understand the course materials. The team offers informed discussion of the effectiveness of exercises and assignments. Although the front-end costs of implementing this system are relatively high, the rewards can be significant. Once you get beyond the stage of initial design and installation, I think you will find the students enthusiastically maintaining the process. A cautionary note:

the mechanics of selecting students to serve on the team are critical. How do you ensure representativeness? Volunteers? Random selection? Rotating seats? Election? What mechanics are necessary to ensure the team is representing the concerns of their classmates?

Because the response to a series of questions like "Was I effective in teaching to your learning style?" will most likely be various forms of bewilderment, I use as many different forms of instruction, assignments, and exercises as possible and carefully monitor students' responses to the various formats. I often make notes on individual student performances in an attempt to detect patterns that may indicate students' preferences.

The joy of investing the time and energy in establishing a continuous classroom assessment process comes from the growth both you and your students will experience as a result of your striving to teach all students equally. One of the keys to making this "painless and seamless" is the passionate support you will get from your students. I find that after my initial discussion with them about my goal of improving their learning experience and the major variables I am concerned about—cultural biases, learning styles, cultural diversity and classroom dynamics, teaching equally, and so on—students are flattered I care enough about their learning to solicit their help in improving my teaching. I am quite candid with my students. I tell them that I am no expert in teaching and learning. I admit that I have never been trained in classroom practices. That I was hired because of my research area and not because of my potential in the classroom. I tell them that if I am to improve their learning, I need to learn from them what methods of instruction work for them and which do not. Once the shock of hearing this disclosure wears off, students accept this responsibility.

Another benefit of this discussion is that it relieves underlying tension and uneasiness that some students may have with others different from themselves. The discussion about cultural diversity, learning styles, cultural hegemony, and unconscious bias removes the hesitancy to address these issues because of the fear of offending a classmate by placing these topics in arena of intellectual exploration. Once this is accepted by the class, I find that their desire to learn from, as well as about, each other conditions their discussions, and self-disclosure becomes commonplace. As a result, students gain the sensibilities of the nature of cultural pluralism.

Teaching students equally takes the drudgery out of teaching. I look forward to each class. I look forward to improving my teaching. The students look forward to improving their learning and teaching me a thing or two. Students of color and others from the margins of our society no longer have to cope with unconscious or conscious discrimination by passively enduring the class period. They become engaged in the learning process as equal participants. It is a joyful experience. It is a symbiotic classroom.

References and Resources

Angelo, T. A., & Cross, K. P. (1993). *Classroom assessment techniques: A handbook for college teachers* (2nd ed.). San Francisco: Jossey-Bass.

Chickering, A., & Gamson, Z. (1987, March). Seven principles for good practice in undergraduate education. *American Association for Higher Education Bulletin*, pp. 3-7.

Davis, B. G. (1993). *Tools for teaching.* San Francisco: Jossey-Bass.

Treisman, U. (1992). Studying students studying calculus: A look at the lives of minority mathematics students in college. *College Mathematics Journal*, 23(5), 362-372.

Treisman, U., & Fullilove, R. (1990). Mathematics achievement among African American undergraduates at the University of California, Berkeley: An evaluation of the mathematics workshop program. *Journal of Negro Education*, 59(3), 463-478.

Treisman, U., & Garland, M. (1993). The mathematics workshop model: An interview with Uri Treisman. *Journal of Developmental Education*, 16(3), 14-16, 18, 20, 22.

4 | Including Multicultural Content and Perspectives in Your Courses

OTIS L. SCOTT

A year ago I was sitting in my office preparing for a meeting when I received a telephone call from a colleague. I could tell from the edge in his voice that he had something important to discuss. "Do you have time to talk about some classroom stuff?" he asked. We arranged to meet that afternoon.

I learned from our meeting that students were raising questions in his government class that were causing him some discomfort. Not because the questions were being raised, but because, as he put it, "I just don't have the background to give responses to questions about subject matter I should know something about." Further, he noted, "My students can tell that I know next to nothing about ethnic groups." What prompted his call to me were questions by students relating to responses by Native Americans and African Americans to the Constitution Convention and how rationalizations supporting slavery and Indian removal could be justified, given the credo of liberty embodied in the Constitution.

After talking for about an hour, my colleague fully understood and willingly agreed to the need to expand the course so as to include more multicultural content. Specifically, this meant initially assigning readings and developing lectures and assignments that brought multicultural perspectives to students. More importantly, this was a new learning approach for him. After our first talk and the many that followed, he has been able to broaden the scope and context of his course in ways that make both him and his course more valuable learning instruments for his students.

I started with this story as a way of establishing a focus for my comments. Over the years I have had similar kinds of experiences, as faculty have recognized the need to broaden their general education courses to include multicultural content. I should add that my colleague is doing just fine with his introductory general education course. Teaching the course continues to be a rewarding experience for all concerned.

What follows is a discussion of some approaches faculty might consider as they undertake the challenges and responsibilities associated with multicultural curriculum revision.

As I earlier indicated, I want to discuss how faculty may go about meeting university requirements calling for the inclusion of multicultural content in their courses. Much of my focus and attention has been directed toward disciplines in the arts, humanities, and social and behavioral sciences. These are disciplinary areas shaping knowledge bases pertinent to my own disciplinary areas: political science, African American studies and ethnic studies. You will find, however, that these general approaches to the inclusion of multicultural content can also be useful in the natural and physical sciences and in the more applied professional curricula such as business and engineering.

Many of us are on campuses that have recently revised general education programs to require all students to take coursework that brings them face to face with the diverse and complex multicultural nature of this nation and the world. Many of us, just as the colleague I described earlier, are challenged to provide learning experiences for our students that explore the experiences and contributions of:

- people of color
- women
- gays and lesbians
- social and religious groups having minority status

Further, some of us are on campuses where students are also required to expand their knowledge of cultures and people outside of the United States.

All of this can be frustrating and otherwise daunting for those of us involved in multicultural curriculum revision. The challenges involved include:

- revising extant course(s) to bring them into compliance with new multicultural requirements
- developing new courses reflecting multicultural content
- conducting research in order to identify appropriate new content
- reexamining our discipline in order to determine the best instructional use of the new content
- becoming both familiar and comfortable with multicultural content
- experimenting with pedagogies that best use the new content

Approaches to Curriculum Revision

Because most of us are trained in the canons of our disciplines, we are strongly inclined to preserve that which we know and profess. We are comfortable with our knowledge of knowledge. As new knowledge is presented, our initial approach is to assay the new data as to the extent to which it can fit into the old (time-tested and true) information shaping the discipline, or subspecialty, or branch of the discipline. If we can use it, we use it. As long as it is not inconvenient or does not present an impediment to what we have always done. This being the case, our approach to the inclusion of multicultural content is likely to follow this well-worn path. The pattern I am referring to is quite simply the additive approach to course revision. It is one of two principle methods to course revision I will introduce here. The two are (a) the additive approach— sometimes glibly referred to as "mix, stir, and serve" and (b) the integrative approach, which involves integrating a multicultural approach to teaching and learning into the entire content of the course.

The Additive Approach to Curriculum Change

This is perhaps the simplest way of responding to the need to include multicultural content into an existing course. One need only to add, for example, Leslie Silko's (1977) *Ceremony*, and James Baldwin's (1963) *The Fire Next Time* to a course on literature in the United States and presto, the course has been transformed. On occasion, texts representing the perspectives of marginalized and excluded groups are not added to the reading list at all. The instructor merely makes mention of the names of a sprinkling of women and people of color. Usually those mentioned are entertainers, athletes, or well-known political figures. The likes of Gloria Estefan, Bill Cosby, Michael Jordan, Michael Jackson, Ben Nighthorse Campbell, Robert Matsui, Henry Cisneros, and Carol Mosley Braun become the archetypes of success for ethnic groups and women.

This approach can be an important first step along the road to curriculum revision. The additive approach also:

- evidences an awareness on the part of the instructor that curriculum change is needed
- begins the process of intellectually reengaging the canon
- prompts the instructor to actively seeking resources and supports
- expands the content of the course to include new information

However, although this approach to curricular change can be a beginning to a much more substantive revision project, too often the more intensive interaction between the instructor and the discipline does not occur. The additive approach becomes both a beginning and the end—a be-all and end-all. Major shortcomings of this approach are:

- The core course remains intact; its "truths" are not substantially challenged, if at all.
- Too often only superficial attention is given to ethnic "stars" and personalities.
- The products of culture (e.g., artifacts, dance, music) are given more meaning than the people or their histories.
- The real meaning—the historical context of the experiences of ethnic groups, women, gays, and lesbians, for example, is not explored. We risk not learning about the struggles for inclusion, dignity and citizenship which shape the experience of marginalized social and religious groups in this society.
- The new content has the appearance of an add-on, something apart from what is considered more privileged information and content.

I recognize that my comments here are practically an indictment of the additive approach. I admit to being wary, if not a bit suspicious of this approach. This is because it does not stretch us far enough as teachers and intellectuals. Moreover, this approach does not make our courses as inclusive of the range of human intellectual traditions as they could be.

If you remember my little anecdote at the beginning of this piece, you might then recall that what my colleague was really looking for was additional information which could be included in his course. This was his pressing need; I strongly suspect that this is the pressing need of most faculty starting out of the gate.

The central questions raised by faculty starting out are, "Where can I find the information?" and "How can I use the information once I get it?" These concerns are addressed by the additive approach and, just as importantly, the immediate concerns regarding new content are also addressed. As initially helpful as this rather practical approach to multicultural course revision may be, I believe that there is a better approach to curriculum change.

The Integrative Approach to Curriculum Change

This approach is intended to bring about significant changes in both what is taught and how it is taught. In effect, this approach results, over time, in such a substantial change in the course content and instructional methods that a new core of information is generated and taught. This approach to curriculum revision is purposeful. It is undertaken with the intent of including multicultural perspectives as part of the course content. This approach is evident not in an added line or section to the syllabus dealing with "non-Western perspectives." The integrative approach is characterized by a richness of non-Western perspectives interwoven throughout the course content.

This emergence of the new core will not be immediate; it is the function of what is likely to be a series of protracted—trial and error—iterations. The key distinction to this approach is the willful attempt to transform the existing core body of knowledge into a multicultural core. As already mentioned, this is an evolutionary process and therefore necessarily requires a commitment of time.

A warning here must also be issued. What I am proposing requires a willingness to raise some fundamental questions about the courses we teach if not the disciplines we profess. These are not easy questions to raise. They are not easy because the order of interrogation I am urging is iconoclastic. A genuine approach to engaging the core knowledge constituting a course or discipline is in some respects akin to smashing sacred idols, or perhaps on a more mischievous note, stealing the emperor's clothing. Neither of these activities is taken kindly by the faculty, who pride themselves as gatekeepers of knowledge—or more properly put, gatekeepers of dominant society perspectives and values. For new faculty these challenges can, and in fact do, present serious problems. On many occasions faculty have had their attempts to achieve retention, promotion, and tenure frustrated and dashed due to their curriculum revision activities, which are perceived to stray from the "traditional." The course approval bureaucracy is also often strewn with pitfalls, as faculty seek acceptance of the course from colleagues sitting on key university committees. Remember my colleague? One of his concerns—and he is not a junior faculty member—related to how his department chair and curriculum committee would respond to his inclusion of a speech by Black Elk and essays by Anna Julia Cooper and Michelle Cliff in his class on U. S. government and politics.

Steps Toward Curriculum Integration

I previously suggested that a crucial first step towards bringing about curriculum change is to engage or reengage the content that one has typically taught in a course. I believe this is an essential activity that should characterize our continuing efforts to remain current in our fields. The kind of interrogation I am referring to involves faculty raising questions as to the extent to which our courses provide students with multicultural learning experiences. A key question may be asked: Does my course assist students with understanding the nature and context of a multicultural society and their roles in this society? More discrete sets of questions may be raised given the general education standards and expectations of courses meeting this requirement. I would think that at a minimum faculty would be prompted to raise the following questions respecting their own course(s):

1. Does my course assist students with knowing the multicultural context of this society?

2. Does this course assist students with knowing major perspectives, views, and frames of reference contributed by diverse social groups to cultural thought and practice?

3. After taking my course will students know of the contributions by women, people of color, and other groups to the institutional life of this nation?

4. After my course will students know more about the major controversies and issues shaping the experiences of ethnic groups?

5. Does my course assist students with an understanding of the synthetic nature of knowledge and that knowledge results from a confluence of intellectual and creative pursuits from diverse human groups?

Of course the key methodological question is: How do I set about doing the actual work of integrating multicultural content into my course regimen? What is the first step to initiating the actual mechanics of change once I have held a self-directed discourse about the objectives and pedagogy of my course? I believe that for most of us, the first lines of assistance are found in our own backyard, among faculty colleagues on our own respective campuses.

Faculty Resources

Over the last generation, many universities have instituted ethnic studies and women's studies programs. Most of these programs have full-time faculty, either as joint appointments with another program or with full appointment lines in ethnic studies or women's studies. These faculty are valuable resources and should be consulted. They can assist with:

- identifying resources, such as bibliographies, articles, media aids and so on
- providing critical feedback on curriculum change activities
- providing comment on issues relating to classroom pedagogy

- constituting a collegial network within which the important work of curriculum change can be nurtured

On some campuses a formalized ethnic studies or women's studies program may not exist. But all is not lost. It is likely that there are faculty—at least one—in history, sociology, anthropology, humanities, literature, the arts, science, mathematics, or the professional fields, for example, who have been doing multicultural teaching and who may be a valuable resource to you in your efforts to revise your course.

If I were to offer some general advice regarding where to begin the hands-on process of curriculum change it would be:

- Seek out nearby faculty resources. This may mean consulting with faculty teaching at institutions near yours if assistance is not immediately available on your campus.
- Attempt to construct a faculty collaboration network as part of the change process.
- Expect to move slowly and incrementally. Reengaging the core discipline is a painstaking process; integrating multicultural perspectives and content into the core is a protracted process.

Using Multicultural Resource Materials

Let us assume you are ready to begin revising the course and that you have a couple of faculty who have agreed to provide assistance as needed in your venture.

What does one begin revising? My suggestion is that even before the actual work of course revision or course development begins, it is imperative that we learn more about the relationship of people of color and women to the discipline we profess. This is an important part of our own education or reeducation process. It is an investment in building our credibility and authority as subject matter experts. It is here that we obtain the background information and perspectives that will enable us to better understand why it is important to incorporate multicultural content into our courses. By engaging this essential first step we put a more solid epistemological grounding under the multicultural project.

Doing this work will necessarily require that faculty in some cases reconstruct the history of the discipline with an eye toward identifying the contributions to it from social groups whose voices have been muted and not heard and whose faces are not seen, even if visible. On this point it is important that faculty not overlook some valuable print resources in this effort to learn more about—or relearn—their discipline.

Resources which may prove helpful will include:

- publications of caucus groups within professional associations, for example, the women's caucus, La Raza caucus, African American caucus, gay/lesbian caucus, Asian American and Native American caucuses
- publications of ethnic studies and women's studies associations
- publications of scholars within the discipline on the subject of multiculturalism and diversity
- publications by ethnic studies and women's studies scholars

The point here is that the initial step to revising the course requires knowing something about the history of the discipline and multiculturalism.

This approach has utility for every discipline. In this regard, I am recommending that all faculty interested in multicultural course revision engage their discipline first. And do so with the intent of identifying the extent to which multicultural perspectives have influenced the development and direction of the discipline. This approach to multicultural revision can be undertaken across disciplines as it lends itself to research and discovery tools particular to each faculty's discipline and specialty. In sum, I am suggesting that the initial approach to curriculum change is not simply limited to one disciplinary area.

In fact, faculty planning to revise or develop a course might initially develop several lectures to be presented periodically throughout the course which demonstrate multicultural perspectives.

This approach to course revision at least begins to place the faculty in an investigative and an interrogative posture vis-à-vis the discipline. As has been stated previously, this is an important first step. It is the beginning of a longer change process where the faculty begins to look at the course with an attitude fixed on content revision which transcends simply tacking new content to the old. The emphasis here is on transforming the core by expanding its composition.

A Curriculum Model: Beyond the Canon

On the subject of curriculum models which may be helpful in our efforts to redesign our courses, I want to describe one that I have been involved with on my campus.

I believe there are aspects of the project which can be borrowed and adapted by faculty. Broadly speaking, the project, entitled "Beyond the Canon: New Strategies for Pedagogy and Curriculum Change," is codirected by Professor Janelle Reinelt and me and is a multicultural curriculum revision project.

The essence of the project is its collaborative feature; faculty work in interdisciplinary teams in order to assist faculty interested in including multicultural content in a targeted general education course. This is a year-long project involving three groups of faculty in intensive curriculum revision activities. It is the collaborative aspect of the program that I believe can be readily adapted by faculty in any department at any campus.

The collaboration involves:

Change Agent Faculty: faculty with multicultural teaching experience and preparation

Target Faculty: faculty wishing to incorporate multicultural content in a general education course

Resource Faculty: faculty having multicultural teaching experience who are typically subject matter experts; they are available as consultants to either or both change agent and target faculty

Change agent and target faculty work together to revise general education courses taught by the target faculty. Some of the typical activities in the collaboration include:

- regular meetings between the dyad (change agent and target faculty) where issues relating to teaching, multiculturalism, diversity, and other matters are discussed
- exchange of journal articles, books, and other resource materials
- trial lectures and class visitation exchanges
- monthly meetings with the entire project faculty during which issues relating to project activities are discussed

There is a summary observation I would like to make about the project which may be helpful if you plan to develop your own. As you might have guessed, most of the target faculty are just like the colleague I referred to at the beginning of this discussion—they first want to add multicultural content. It is a bit simplistic to say they all are looking for a "quick fix": Some are, some aren't.

What we do notice is that over the year-long project, the core of the discipline or the canon is engaged. Most faculty arrive at the point where they understand that simply adding Denise Chavez and Amy Tan to a course on major women writers is hardly transformative. And yet, the addition is an important triggering activity; it begins the transformative process.

Including multicultural content is never a quick fix or an end. It is an ongoing process that necessarily involves making a serious examination of the intellectual scaffolding underlying the canon.

The Rewards of Our Labor

As challenging and fraught with difficulties as multicultural curriculum change can be, it can also be intellectually stimulating and rewarding. As teachers we are involved in a most important enterprise. We are major participants in a social activity that is intended to shape and frame a reality or sets of realities for our students. We provide our students with both bases of knowledge and skills which will enable them to understand, manipulate, and change their realities. We want our students to be vital participants in their environments, not bumps on a log. To this end, education which includes multicultural learning experiences is vital. We provide students with the ability to better understand the culturally diverse national and international societies they simultaneously inhabit. This is a tremendous responsibility that must be mutually shared by ourselves and our students. The classroom is an important venue within which we can take the first step toward meeting this responsibility.

References and Resources

Baldwin, J. (1963). *The fire next time*. New York: Dial Press.

Banks, J. A. (1990). *Teaching strategies for ethnic studies* (5th ed.). Boston: Allyn & Bacon.

Bergquist, W. H., Gould, R. R., & Greenberg, E. M. (1981). *Designing undergraduate education*. San Francisco: Jossey-Bass.

Boyer, E. L. (1987). *College: The undergraduate experience in America*. New York: Harper & Row.

Cheng, L. L. (1990). Recognizing diversity. *American Behavioral Scientist, 34*(2), 263-278.

Cortes, C. E. (1983, April). Multiethnic and global education: Partners for the eighties? *Phi Delta Kappan*, pp. 568-571.

Gaff, J. G. (1983). *General education today: A critical analysis of controversies, practices, and reforms*. San Francisco: Jossey-Bass.

Gay, G. (1983, April). Multiethnic education: Historical developments and future prospects. *Phi Delta Kappan*, 560-563.

Hayden, T. (1985). *California higher education: The challenge of the 21st century*. Sacramento: State of California Assembly Subcommittee on Higher Education.

Hoover, M. (1990). Ethnic studies in the university. *American Behavioral Scientist, 34*(2), 251-262.

Rothenberg, P. S. (Ed.). (1992). *Race, class, and gender in the United States*. New York: St. Martin's Press.

Schlesinger, A. M. (1992). *The disuniting of America*. New York: Norton.

Silko, L. M. (1977). *Ceremony*. New York: Viking Press.

Simonson, R., & Walker, S. (Eds.). (1988). *Multicultural literacy*. St. Paul, MN: Graywolf Press.

Woodson, C. G. (1922). *Miseducation of the Negro*. New York: AMS Press.

5 | Languages and Cultures in the Classroom

ANN M. JOHNS

Our languages and academic experiences affect our teaching; likewise, our students' languages and academic experiences affect their learning. Our diverse students come to our classes with rich linguistic and schooling experiences. The more we know about these experiences, the better we can understand their responses and perhaps modify our teaching practices and assessment accordingly.

I have studied and taught in several cultures and attempted several languages; thus I have accumulated my own collection of experiences that have influenced my current teaching and assessment practices. For example, when I spent a year on a Fulbright Grant in China, I gave a number of lectures to my students, practicing teachers of English as a Foreign Language. While lecturing in the United States to American-born students, I gauge interest by the number of thoughtful questions that follow my formal presentation. However, in China, if a listener poses a question, it is considered to be an attack upon the perfection of the speaker's lecture. Following my lectures there, complete silence reigned. The only way I could entice my students into posing questions was to explain my expectations and to give points for every relevant question asked.[1] Many Asian American students in the United States are still influenced by the "silence" tradition: They are very uncomfortable with question-posing or critique, especially of people with higher status.

In Egypt, where I was a university instructor for two years, I made a different discovery about lectures. Cairo lecture classes are often very large (500-1,000), and lecturers speak while students talk in groups, read *El-Ahram* (the official newspaper), and walk in and out of the classroom.[2]

In both China and Egypt, and among a variety of other cultures, the purposes for reading—and the approaches to processing texts—are quite different from our preferred practices. Reading aloud (e.g., from the Koran) is required for basic literacy in most Muslim cultures and continues to be practiced in many academic contexts among Muslim students.[3] Again, we have evidence of the same approaches in the United States. Shirley Brice Heath (1984) tells us that in many cultures in this country, reading aloud is much more highly prized than silent reading. (And speaking well is more highly prized than writing well.)

Memorization—to repeat or regurgitate in writing, verbatim—is also common practice in many school cultures. This practice continues to be employed by some of our own students, as well. In some cases, as I found in my interviews with a Vietnamese American undergraduate biology student, memorization and regurgitation pays off, especially when bilingual students must respond rapidly in a timed essay examination.

Needs Assessment and Ongoing Class Evaluation

How do we investigate the previous classroom and literacy experiences of our students? One way is to begin with a standard needs assessment, such as the one instituted in our university's biology program. (See Appendix.)

If we want to more thoroughly examine literacy and language practices and how they affect student work, we may need to consult literacy sources (e.g., Dubin & Kuhlman, 1992; Murray, 1992; Scarcella, 1990) or the faculty, staff, or students on our campuses who can provide insights. Some questions that the literature poses about student classroom cultures are listed in Table 5.1.

Another possibility for investigating language and literacy practices involves direct questions to students, a practice that I have instituted in all of my classes. Table 5.2 suggests some of these questions.

The answers to the questions in Table 5.1 and Table 5.2 have proved useful to me as an instructor. For example, if I have a considerable number of students who do not speak English as a first language, I invite them to tape the classes (because I seem to be unable to speak slowly). I also discuss answers to the bio-data questions with all the students, so that they can appreciate the diversity of the class.

The content and strategy questions also assist me, not only to plan, but to give students the impression, which I hope is true, that the class is theirs, designed to present concepts and information and to assess them in a manner that is most appropriate.

As the class progresses, I find that it is valuable to periodically "test the waters," that is, to ask students to evaluate the class informally. This practice is especially useful for those students whose cultures prohibit open criticism of my classroom practices. Evaluation can be accomplished in a variety of ways, for example, through group discussion and report or through student written commentary.

After completing an examination, I might ask students: How well did you do? To what do you attribute your success and failures? Did you attempt to translate from your first language as you wrote? What strategies did you use in approaching the test; for example, did you read it all first and then choose the questions to answer?[4]

After completing an assignment I would ask: What did you learn about the assignment you just completed? How will you

Table 5.1 Questions About Student Classroom Cultures and Behaviors

---

1. What are some of the features of the school cultures from which our students come?

What are the dominant teacher/student roles?
Is the teacher expected to be the authority on all issues?
Are students encouraged to take an active part in the classroom discussion?
What are accepted gender relationships within classrooms?

---

2. With what student-student relationships are our students familiar?

Have they been grouped with students from cultures other than their own?
Is working independently or in groups valued?

---

3. What are the "classroom manners" with which the students are familiar?

What rules about criticism of other students or teachers are they comfortable with?
How close do people in classrooms stand to each other?
Do they touch?
How are students accustomed to responding to lectures?

---

4. What were the roles of reading, writing, and assessment in the students' earlier school contexts?

Reading
Did reading mean memorizing? Reading aloud?
For what reasons did students read? To remember? To analyze? To critique?
Writing
How much writing in English have students completed?
How much writing have they experienced in their first languages?
What problems do they face when writing in a second language or in standard academic dialect?
In what genres have they written?
How has their writing been evaluated?
What is the role of copying from texts in their previous writing experiences?

---

approach the next assignment differently? What practices will you continue? If you were an instructor designing the next assignment for this course, what would you keep the same? What would you change? Why?

Table 5.2 Questions About Content and Strategies

Content Questions:
(Students work in groups to formulate answers.)

1. The name of this class is _____ .
   How would you explain the class title to your parents or a younger
      brother or sister?
2. What do people in this discipline study?
3. What topics may be covered in this class?
4. Have you ever read a book or article about _____ ?
   If so, what was discussed?
5. Why did you enroll in this course?
6. What questions would you like this class to answer for you?

Pedagogical/School Culture Questions:
(Students answer individually.)

1. How do you learn most effectively? For example, do you like to work
      in groups? Why or why not?
2. What helps you to remember? For example, do you write things down,
      say them aloud to yourself, or rehearse them with a friend?
3. Do you think that you take good lecture notes?
   If not, what presents difficulty for you?
4. Have most of your classes been lecture classes?
   If so, what do you see as the strengths or weaknesses of lectures?
5. Do you like to ask questions in class?
   If so, why? If not, why not?

Learning/Assessment Questions:
(Answer either individually or in groups.)

1. What have instructors in previous classes done to enhance your
      understanding of courses or to improve your motivation?
2. When instructors have given writing assignments, have they provided
      models of previous student work and given specific grading criteria?
3. How have they helped you with the reading? For example, have they
      provided pre-reading questions, guiding you in your approach to the
      assigned texts?
4. How have instructors helped you to do your best on examinations?
   For example, have they given you examples of good examination
      responses and discussed why they are good?

Evaluation should also involve students' comments about
the content. In one class on my campus, for example, after
completing each assigned reading, students are required to

write a question about the reading. Then they write a second question that links all of their reading questions from previous classes. The faculty member collects the questions and reads a few, commenting on what further questions might be asked. This practice ensures that students complete the reading, forces them to write (but not oppressive amounts), and is a continual source of materials for group work.[5]

A friend of mine recommends a "pouring down words" session, which I have instituted. Once a month or so, students devote 10 minutes at the end of the hour to writing an unsigned commentary on the class: how it's taught, how it's going for them; what they like or think is unfair, and so on. During the next period, I read some of the remarks, both positive and negative, particularly those that I plan to act on.

I find that these ongoing evaluation approaches help me to understand better the cultures and strategies of the students whom I am teaching. They assist me in understanding what my students have learned and what they haven't and whether their reading is effective. The approaches also assist me in recognizing factors in the class dynamic of which I am not otherwise aware; for example, that a student has lost face because I criticized her openly, or that one student is dominating a group or a lecture session.

Group Work

Although I find that for school culture reasons, group work is not always easy to implement in classrooms, I still advocate the use of groups, especially in large classes. Sometimes, the reasons for resistance to groups are local ones; juniors and seniors have become accustomed over the years to sitting in large lecture halls and "going into automatic pilot," so they object to the active nature of group participation. As I indicated earlier, other reasons may stem from first culture experiences. Students may believe that the teacher should be the only authority and thus they cannot learn from other students. They may not want to associate with students from the cultures represented in their assigned groups.[6] They may believe that group members' (or their own) English is not adequate for group discussion. However, each of these objections can be countered, especially if there are students within the class who are comfortable with group work and provide leadership.

Other students object if the group work and projects are not well structured—and in this, they are absolutely right. Groups cannot be effective if they are simply told to discuss a topic in some general way. Students must be given a relevant task or problem that they can solve and report on, something that doesn't necessarily have a correct answer but is central to class concepts, content, and assessment.

Therefore, there are several important considerations in maintaining group work: students in groups must be willing to work together, and they must do so fairly often; they must understand the value—as well as the limitations—of group work; the groups must be well-structured; and the tasks for the groups must be important to the goals of the class.

Fortunately, many sources exist to assist us in establishing and maintaining groups. In this book, Chapter 3 by Ray Lou and Chapter 6 by Olita D. Harris contain further ideas and suggestions for managing group work.

Though there are many possibilities mentioned in the literature, I have been most successful with establishing permanent four- or five-person groups of mixed linguistic and cultural backgrounds. The groups meet at least every other week in class, and if they choose to do so, they also meet outside of class (for study purposes, generally). The groups are structured: Each student has a role (discussion leader, recorder, facilitator, expert), and the roles are rotated weekly so that everyone has several opportunities to take each role. Groups meet for short periods of time (20 minutes) during which they solve ungraded problems relating to the lectures or critique each other's writing or presentations.[7] I am very careful to make the issues and problems discussed by groups central to topics on my examinations.

Students benefit from group work in a number of ways. They must be active, so presumably, they will learn more. They find support and cohesion among class members whom they had not known and might not have associated with outside of class.[8] They exchange phone numbers and contact each other for class notes or when one group member is absent. They begin to study together outside of class, and sometimes they form friendships that last throughout their university careers. They gain confidence in dealing with the subject matter and their ability to critique each other and class materials. Nonetheless, problems may arise: There may be one uncooperative or overbearing student who destroys the group dynamic; students may drop the class, resulting in a smaller cohort. In addition, if tasks for the groups are not well-constructed, students are confused and time is wasted. I must admit, it's easier to lecture.

Writing-to-Learn

Writing-to-learn (WTL) has been one of the key elements in the Writing-Across-the-Curriculum (WAC) movement for a number of years (see, e.g., Fulweiler & Young, 1986). WAC proponents argue that when students write, they can think through ideas, organize their thoughts, and expand their abilities to critique. There are other advantages to WTL, as well. When I give a WTL task in my class, every student must be involved. No one can slough off or sleep in the back of the room. WTL experiences also provide writing practice in nonthreatening situations; thus, my students who are more accustomed to other writing systems[9] are given opportunities just to practice writing in English.

In Table 5.3, I present one WTL possibility, the Quick Write, which has been very popular in my WAC workshops.

Modeling

The university culture is often mysterious to our students; for, as I mentioned earlier, it may be considerably different

Table 5.3 The Quick Write

This is a brief, ungraded response to a question. It is employed for a variety of purposes, two of which are suggested:

To Introduce a Concept

As the class opens, I ask students to begin in their notes with a sketchy written piece. Here are my instructions: "You have just read about x. You have 3 minutes to write down everything you remember about it: its definition, an example, and its relationship to other concepts in the course. Your writing will not be collected or even seen by anyone else, so don't worry about correct spelling or punctuation. Write in lists if that helps you."

I time the students carefully; and, after 3 minutes, they work in pairs to read their responses aloud. Then I ask several pairs of students to report on some of the information they share in their quick writes. Following, this, I proceed with the lecture on the topic.

To Summarize

After completing a portion of a lecture or group discussion, I ask the students to summarize what they have heard, using their notes as guides. When they're finished, I select several confident students and ask them to read their summaries to the class. Other students then compare what these students have presented with their own summaries and notes, commenting on what is missing, what is overemphasized and other factors. This exercise gives me some indication of what students understood and what they didn't. It also reveals a great deal about note taking, which some students find to be very difficult. Sometimes I vary this WTL approach by asking all of the students to turn in their summaries (unsigned) so that I can look them over briefly and compare them with my expectations.

from their own school or home cultural experiences. Thus, I find that modeling for the students the texts and practices of my classroom assists them in understanding how to study and what is important to the class.

Research indicates that many students do not know how to approach the reading of a textbook; they have even more difficulty when reading authentic texts of a discipline, for example, historiography or ethnographies. For many students, the reading process is always the same: Read the first word of the text, then the second word. . . . My bilingual students devote hours to looking up every word they don't know, failing to distinguish between those words that are important to the topic and those that are not.

Faculty can assist students by demonstrating to them how they, themselves, approach the reading of assigned texts. For example, they can indicate that they skim the text first to discover how it's organized before reading some sections more carefully. They can show students how to use the "aids" (e.g., the questions at the end of the chapter or chapter summaries). And most importantly, they can demonstrate how the readings should be exploited for the purposes of the class. Are they a supplement to the lecture or laboratory? If so, how should they be read? How would the instructors read these texts to prepare for examinations?

Faculty can also assist students by demonstrating their examination grading processes. For example, are they very much influenced by the first sentence a student writes in a response? How do they use grading criteria in this processing?

Many bilingual students have very little experience with writing, either in their first or second languages. Thus, when they are given a writing assignment, they often have no idea what their texts should look like and why. Some faculty place on reserve good examples of student responses to the same assignment.[10] Or, they ask all students to buy a packet of materials that includes at least two examples of student papers. Class time can be well spent on working through these papers, discussing the format, the style, the methodology, the content, the introduction of concepts or any other issues germane to the assignment and the goals of the class.

Distributing a list of specific criteria for grading will also assist students in writing their papers or studying for examinations. If they know that 15% of the grade is based upon editing a paper, they will edit. If they know that the paper must be organized in a specific way or must draw from a minimum number of sources, many will do as assigned.

When I suggest these modeling approaches to faculty, some protest that these kinds of exercises take time away from covering content. They also argue that if they tell students all of this, then the students won't be challenged, for the faculty are, in effect, "giving away the store." I argue that spending some time on text forms and the values that drive texts in a discipline is a matter of initiation and not giving away the store. Adopting these practices may also result in better student papers and grades.

Portfolio Assessment

Finally I consider an alternative to single, timed, in-class examinations, the latter of which, as I have mentioned earlier, are not the most effective tools for evaluating linguistically diverse students.

Portfolio assessment has caused considerable interest on my campus and elsewhere, for it provides opportunities for students and faculty to integrate curriculum and assessment in a coherent manner. If carefully planned, portfolios allow for student input and reflection, acknowledge the value of their first languages and cultures, and provide opportunities for students to demonstrate their abilities to complete a variety of tasks under a number of conditions. Portfolios also give instructors insight into students' abilities and problems; and, finally, they allow for more interesting grading experiences for faculty.

A full discussion of portfolios cannot appear here; however, in the references, and in Chapter 6 of this book, there are volumes listed that can be consulted for a more complete presentation. A brief outline of the features that portfolios share is contained in Box 5.1.

Portfolios can be designed for a variety of purposes. On my campus, for example, a history instructor asks students to develop entries relating to pedagogy for future teachers; in chemistry, a faculty member requires a theme-based portfolio ("to encourage students to see the relationship between man [sic] and the ocean"); in social work, students keep portfolios in all core classes to measure their professional development;

Box 5.1

Portfolios Defined

Portfolios are:

Collections, representing students' work over time

An example of the "over time" feature is the extensive portfolio required of future teachers at San Diego State University. These students must keep a portfolio that integrates their classwork throughout their entire undergraduate career.

Representative of central class goals

For example, if summary, analysis, synthesis, or definition are important goals for students, then entries in the portfolio should represent these goals. If a particular approach to a topic is a class goal, then this can be represented in one of the papers.

Selected items

Entries in portfolios are few (five maximum) for a term. The instructor determines entry type; however, either the students or the instructor may decide which examples of this type are included in the portfolio.

Opportunities for reflection

An important element in portfolios is the issue of student reflection. For example, if students include one of their essay examination responses in the portfolio, then this should be accompanied by a reflection, answering such questions as: Why is this a good essay response? Did it answer the question well? What important content does it include?

in classics, students compile cumulative portfolios in their major; in education, portfolios are designed to strengthen the reading/writing connection.

One important aspect of portfolios is their versatility, not only in terms of class goals, but for purposes of assessment. Thus, they are of particular value to the diverse, multilingual student who may have difficulty writing under pressure. Under most portfolio systems, the student is given time to assemble a number of entries and reflect upon them, thus providing for the instructor a more comprehensive view of student work.

Before leaving the topic of portfolios, a complex approach that must be examined with more care than can be afforded here, I would like to turn again to student reflection. As mentioned earlier, one central feature of portfolios is that students have an opportunity to reflect upon their reading, their writing, their learning and test-taking, and upon other issues, as well.

Table 5.4 provides a few possibilities that are currently used for questions to begin student reflection.

Students keep portfolios throughout the semester (or longer, as required), accumulating entries and reflections. The entries are indexed, bound in a small notebook and submitted to the instructor, who may grade them in a manner such as this: The portfolio represents 50% of the class grade; of that proportion, 25% is awarded for completion of the portfolio and 25% for the reflections.

It goes without saying that the possibilities for scoring and entries are infinite. However, the results will be the same: Students will feel a sense of ownership; they will be able to develop an awareness of their own progress and difficulties and of the various strengths and interests that they bring to class.

Increasing Student Involvement and Investment

I have mentioned here a number possibilities for transformations that can enhance learning and encourage the involvement of linguistically diverse students and, not incidentally,

Table 5.4 Portfolio Reflection Questions

After Including an Assignment as a Portfolio Entry:

Why did you include this assignment?

What are the particularly good aspects of this assignment?

How was it important to your learning in this class?

How does what you have read or experienced assist you in completing this assignment? For example, did your knowledge of other languages help you? Were you assisted by your knowledge of your own culture and traditions?

How is this assignment different from earlier assignments given (or from assignments in other classes)? For example, are the steps in completing this assignment different? Is the formatting unusual? If so, why?

After Including a Test:

Why did you choose this test to include in your portfolio?

What does it show about the criteria for grading in this class?

What does it show about your writing quality or understanding of the class content?

What does it show about what you learned from group sessions?

After Including a WTL Entry:

Why did you choose this ungraded writing for your portfolio?

What does it show about your growth as a student?

What does it show about your writing in English?

What does it tell the instructor about your abilities and interests?

---

make our teaching more rewarding. I do not suggest that an instructor contemplating change adopt all of these possibilities at the same time. Instead, the most appealing approach for faculty or students could be attempted over the period of several semesters, so that the problems inherent in the approach can be solved.

What I have suggested may benefit all students; however, bilingual and multilingual students for whom our classroom cultures are particularly foreign may benefit most. This has been my experience, and I hope that readers will share it.

Notes

1. It was difficult for them, even then, since question-posing in English is very complex. If only we had a nice tag, like the French "n'est-ce pas?" to insert at the end of statements. In Chinese, questioning is even easier: you just add the question particle *ma* to a statement.

2. One reason for this, I discovered, is that instructors sell their lecture notes on the side. Variations on this practice, that is, sale of notes, exist in the United States, of course.

3. As it is in China for very different reasons. While in Shanghai, we lived near the university where I worked. Often, we would be awakened as students read aloud from their texts, walking slowly across the playing fields.

4. One of my graduate students interviewed expert and novice student test-takers in a psychology class. She found that the experts initially skimmed the entire examination, planned carefully , urged themselves on, and did not spend much time on those questions that they could not answer.

5. I am indebted to Frank Stites, professor of history, for this suggestion. (Professor Stites is frequently honored as outstanding faculty member by students in his department.)

6. I had an unfortunate experience with this in one of my classes. After I had grouped my students, many of whom were Southeast Asian, one student remained, sitting alone. I asked members of his group why he wasn't included, and they were surprised that I didn't understand and accept their exclusionary practices. "Why, he's Cambodian," they said.

7. Unless students are sold on the value of some of these activities, the class attendance on group days may go down. In a history class on my campus, for example, only one third of the students showed up for peer critiques of papers when that activity was announced in advance.

8. Some very interesting results can accrue from cultural mixes. One of my Chicano students, for example, was delighted to get to know a Palestinian. "You know, Dr. J.," he said, "I've discovered in this class that there are many oppressed people in the world." This was a more important discovery for this student than anything I could teach him.

9. The writing systems issue is a crucial one. As a person who has attempted to write Arabic and Chinese, I can understand how difficult it must be for our students to convert to English from Cambodian (Khmer), Hebrew, and a number of languages with very different writing systems.

10. When I suggested putting good papers on library reserve, some faculty sent their undergraduates to the best journals in their discipline to see how writing should be done. The students were overwhelmed and became very discouraged about ever being able to write a satisfactory paper for the class. For these reasons, I recommend using student papers, which

though flawed, may appear to be within the realm of possibility for the class. Using papers by bilingual and other diverse students is a very good idea, I have found.

References and Resources

Belanoff, P., & Dickson, M. (Eds.). (1991). *Portfolios: Process and product.* Portsmouth, NH: Heinemann/Boynton-Cook. (A collection of articles on portfolios in writing and content classes.)

Christenbury, L., & Kelly, P. P. (1983). *Questioning: A path to critical thinking.* Urbana IL: NCTE/ERIC. (A nice, short volume on positing questions: good for group exercises.)

Diamond, R. M. (1989). *Designing and improving courses and curricula in higher education.* San Francisco: Jossey-Bass. (A complete guide to redesigning a curriculum.)

Dubin, N., & Kuhlman, N. (Eds.). (1992). *Cross-cultural literacy: Global perspectives on reading and writing.* Englewood Cliffs, NJ: Regents/Prentice Hall. (An informative collection on academic literacy practices throughout the world.)

Friere, P. (1970). The "banking" concept of education. In *The pedagogy of the oppressed* (Myra B. Ramos, Trans.). New York: Continuum. (A classic that many of you know.)

Fulweiler, T., & Young, A. (Eds.). (1986). *Writing across the disciplines: Research into practice.* Upper Montclair, NJ: Boynton/Cook. (Edited by two WAC gurus, this collection includes a number of interesting articles on pedagogy.)

Graves, D. H., & Sunstein, B. S. (1992). *Portfolio portraits.* Portsmouth, NJ: Heinemann/Irwin. (A collection of articles on portfolios; good, practical suggestions.)

Heath, S. B. (1984). *Ways with words: Language, life and work in communities and classrooms.* Cambridge: Cambridge University Press. (A classic discussion of the uses of literacy in a variety of American cultures.)

Holt, D. D. (Ed.). (1993). *Cooperative learning: A response to linguistic and cultural diversity.* McHenry, IL: Delta Systems. (Excellent for faculty who are interested in instituting group or pair work.)

Johns, A. M. (1991a). Faculty assessment of ESL student literacy skills: Implications for writing assessment. In L. Hamp-Lyons (Ed.), *Assessing second language writing in academic contexts* (pp. 167-180). Norwood, NJ: Ablex. (After faculty accused my students of being "illiterate," I interviewed them about the features of academic literacy.)

Johns, A. M. (1991b). Interpreting an English competency examination: The frustrations of an ESL science student. *Written Communication, 8,* 379-401. (A case study of a Vietnamese student whose high GPA in biology did not assist him in passing a culturally-biased examination in English.)

Marzano, R., Brandt, R. S., Hughes, C. S., Jones, B. F., Presseisen, B. A., Rankin, S. C., & Cuhor, C. (1988). *Dimensions of thinking: A framework for curriculum and instruction.* Alexandria, VA: Association for Supervision and Curriculum Development. (Defines "thinking" in the disciplines, then provides suggestions for developing critical thought in the classroom.)

Murray, D. E. (1992). *Diversity as a resource: Redefining cultural literacy.* Alexandria, VA: TESOL. (A useful collection for understanding motivations and difficulties of students from a variety of linguistic and ethnic communities.)

San Diego State University, College of Education. (c. 1990). *Portfolio design: A faculty handbook (Celebrating the teacher-scholar).* San Diego: Author. (A basic portfolio guide for faculty.)

Scarcella, R. (1990). *Teaching language minority students in the multicultural classroom.* Englewood Cliffs, NJ: Prentice Hall. (Though written for public school teachers, this text includes a number of chapters that are relevant to college classrooms, as well, e.g., the discussions of literacy and schooling in diverse students' cultures and of incorporation of these languages and cultures in classrooms.)

6 | Equity in Classroom Assessment

OLITA D. HARRIS

In the past, the approaches to education in the United States had their roots in Europe. Concomitantly, much of student outcomes assessment is likewise rooted in those traditions, which value linear learning, causal models, deductive and axiomatic logic, hierarchial social organization, authoritarian ideology, and competitive ethics (Maruyama, 1974). These traditions serve to exclude large numbers of our population. For example, how might an assessment strategy take into account cultural taboos or learning etiquette about eye contact, competition, or "standing out" in any way (Axtell, 1991)? What would be the use of a strategy that requires abstract, integrated approaches in cultural groups where skills are learned through a hands-on approach and one aspect at a time or where learning takes place through an oral tradition? What might we make of the resulting data? To what would our analyses speak?

What appears to be needed at this point is a reconceptualization of assessment to include the multicultural dimensions mentioned above. This reconceptualization begins with the recognition of the demographic shifts occurring in our universities as well as considerations of what will be taught along with who will be taught and how (Kolodny, 1991). Only then can we address the measurement of the educational impact of the class, program, or institution on its students in ways that will be meaningful to the students themselves and the programs that educate them (Terenzini, 1989). In other words, instructional patterns cannot and should not be separated from assessment strategies. This is especially true in the classroom. The key concept in this endeavor is intentionality, that is, the deliberate, thoughtful development of assessment strategies and technologies that allow for the multiplicity of ways in which knowledge and skills can be taught, learned, and judged.

Equity in assessment is an inclusive ethic which by definition shuns and is incompatible with exclusion. In addition, knowledge, like reality, is a social construction and reflects the context in which it resides. The context is the one which results when the culture of the students—all of the students—interacts with the teacher's culture. Both bring language and dialect, nonverbal communications, perspectives and worldviews, behavioral styles and nuances, methods of reasoning and validating knowledge, and cultural identification to the teaching-learning-assessment enterprise. And in the end, all are transformed by it. The culture that is forged from this amalgam has similar meaning for all concerned (Banks, 1986, pp. 21-35). It is neither assimilation nor acculturation but accommodation. This does not mean that allegiance to or identification with anyone's individual culture is denied or denigrated. It does mean, however, that common ground is created wherein interaction can occur that is meaningful to those involved. It also means that assessment and subsequent statements about individual, class, departmental, or institutional effectiveness must take into consideration what students, all students, bring to the institution in the way of cultural imperatives, how those influence learning, the appropriate indicators of change and growth, pertinent data collection strategies, and suitable analyses of the data. Finally, it means that all classroom endeavors should be aimed toward creating a "level playing field." Equity in the teaching/learning endeavor is the logical outcome of this approach.

Equitable assessment strategies must be proactive to have an impact that can be generalized beyond the particular moment and instance. They must be preventive, not merely ameliorative; preventive of the kinds of analyses of students that are negative not because of the students' abilities but because of their reaction to an education that failed to take them into consideration in the teaching/learning equation. For example, making assumptions about a student's apparent lack of attention, or respect, or intelligence because of avoidance of eye contact. For some American Indian and Asian cultures, that is an indicator of deference to an authority figure or elder. However, strategies must also be undergirded and supported by an awareness and analysis of pedagogical options that encompass, frame, and support the variety of ways of knowing, learning, thinking, and problem-solving and the range of worldviews, approaches to life, values, and beliefs.

What I propose are strategies that are suggestive of promising avenues to consider, to follow, and to explore. In addition, they fulfill, to a great degree, the considerations noted above. That is, the techniques and strategies allow the student whose culture demands that he/she not stand out to contribute and actively participate without violating cultural imperatives. The techniques and strategies permit students who are more comfortable with the certainty of numbers than with the ambiguity that often accompanies social discourse to try to apply new knowledge and skills without exposing themselves to what for them can be crushing criticism. For students who are taught that one does not contradict a teacher or anyone in authority, even when questions have not been answered adequately, the techniques and strategies structure an engagement in a dialogue with the professor without the attendant anxiety. The techniques presented here are based on successful strategies used by myself, my colleagues, and others. These strategies include collaborative learning and structured peer feedback approaches, daily learning logs, small groups (for operationalizing concepts), learning files, and minicapstone experiences.

Collaborative Learning
and Structured Peer Feedback

This approach is characterized by the use of small groups—no more than three or four people per group. Larger groups require too much time for too little gain. Also, a larger group tends to inhibit candor and increase anxiety (about standing out, contradicting those in authority, and so on), which effectively decreases the value of the experience. The small group is used to provide feedback about written assignments several weeks before they are due. The objective is to maximize students' learning and improve their writing and critical thinking skills while at the same time allowing them to improve their work in a less threatening atmosphere. It is much easier for students to receive feedback from a peer than from the professor, especially at an early stage of development for the assignment. Also, this strategy reflects the manner in which many cultures conduct their lives on a day-to-day basis. They view the world in terms of the interdependence of its entities. In addition, a number of disciplines value the ability to work cooperatively and collaboratively. The products of these kinds of activities are typically more thoroughly thought out, useful, complete, and creative.

Students are asked to bring two copies of the assignment draft to share in the feedback session. One entire class session is devoted to this process. Students give each group member the draft and each member spends time reading the draft according to criteria delineated in a handout. They are encouraged to make notes on the draft and when all have finished, each in turn provides verbal feedback to the others.

The handout instructs the reader to be as helpful as possible to the author of the draft. The questions (criteria) to guide comments are as follows:

- How complete is the draft? Has the assignment been addressed? What steps should the author take to complete the draft? Be specific.

- Is what is intended clear? Is this draft in an acceptable format (i.e., standard headings, subheadings, references, and citations, etc.)?
- Does the narrative engage the reader? What is the most interesting section of the paper? Why? What makes the other sections less interesting?
- What did you learn from the paper?
- What did you learn about your own writing from reading what others wrote?

Students are given a week to revise their assignments before submitting them to me, along with the original draft, for feedback and suggestions. Students submit all versions and the final paper for grading. They also submit a cover page that addresses the question "What was the most difficult part of the paper to do? Why?" The intent is for them to learn the content of the assignment but also to reflect on the learning about the learning, the meta-analysis, if you will. Students gain insight about their own learning processes and how they approach their work. I gain insight about how well I am communicating the intentions of the course as well as the questions students may still have about the course.

Students' comments about this assignment were uniformly positive with several stating that this was the most valuable learning experience they had had.

Daily Learning Logs

The Learning Log model is a modified version of one shared by a campus colleague and the one developed by Pat Cross and Tom Angelo (1988, pp. 120-123) in their *Classroom Assessment Techniques*. This is a version of the academic journal. See Figure 6.1 for an illustration of the Learning Log.

I have used this process for a number of years and have modified its application over time to make it more useful for students and to provide more accurate feedback about where

Learning Log

Name: _____ Date: _____
Course: _____

PART 1: *Complete this section before the class session.*

How did you prepare for this class session?

Identify three questions you want to have answered related to today's topic.

How will you participate? What will you contribute? How will you get the answers to your questions?

PART 2: *Complete this section at the end of the class session.*

What are the answers to your questions?

What are the three most important things you learned today?

What other questions were generated by today's class discussion?

PART 3: *Complete this section at the end of the class session.*

What interfered with your learning and/or getting your questions answered?

What facilitated your learning and/or getting your questions answered?

What will you do to decrease interference with and increase facilitation of your learning if a similar situation arises again?

How will today's learning affect your out-of-class learning/activities?

Figure 6.1. Learning Log

students are in their learning of the class content. Initially, I instructed students to take 10 minutes at the beginning of class to complete the first part of the log and 15 minutes at the end to complete them. I would then collect them, read them, make comments as needed, and return them at the beginning of the following class session. However, I discovered that portions were left unanswered, and when asked why, students responded that they did not have enough time to complete them. Consequently, I issued students the log for the next class session at the end of the current session. That provided them the time to think about the questions they had regarding the assigned readings as they were reading, and so on. Also, it did not take up any class time. As a result their questions were more pertinent and I obtained a clearer picture of what was on their minds and, perhaps, what I needed to cover in more detail in the next class session. At the same time, I allowed them to complete the second and third parts of the log after class. This permitted them time to think about what they had learned and to determine what they needed to do to facilitate their own learning. The Learning Log allows students to take responsibility for their own learning and provides continuous feedback about the effectiveness of my teaching. In addition, for students who have cultural prohibitions about standing out, it provides them the means for getting their questions answered while, at the same time, encouraging reflection on how their own learning takes place.

As stated previously, I used this with every class session. However, it may be used periodically to spot-check how students are learning. One note of caution is that initially students will attempt to second-guess the instructor—to figure out what they think the instructor wants them to convey. It takes a few sessions for them to understand that this is a learning tool for them and a teaching tool for the instructor. Although the logs are not graded, they do count toward class participation, which typically represents 10% of the final course grade. It is certainly not necessary to include them in calculating any grade, but it helps students to understand that completing the logs has a value. Things that have no extrinsic value usually are not taken seriously, at least initially. It is only later that the intrinsic value of the activity becomes a factor.

Round-Robin Role-Play
for Operationalizing Concepts

Actually, this could be considered another form of collaborative learning. At any rate, it's a tool for students to practice application of concepts in an environment that is safe and in which they receive immediate feedback about the correctness of the application. I call it a round-robin role-play. This is particularly useful in professional programs that involve a high degree of skill development, for example, human service programs and the like. Also, this strategy accommodates students who learn best from a hands-on/application process. Although it may be argued that this is not an assessment strategy, per se, as has been stated previously, to be effective, assessment cannot and should not be separated from teaching. This strategy provides continuous feedback about the level of competence a student achieves as he/she is learning these skills.

The idea is to present a concept, for example, paraphrasing. Using an overhead transparency, I explain what it is, why it is used in client interactions, the situations in which it is commonly used, and then present examples. I also furnish them with a handout containing the same material. Students, in groups of three then take turns applying the concept in a social worker/client situation. For example, Student 1, who is role-playing the client, makes a statement. Student 2, who is role-playing the social worker, paraphrases the statement made by the client. Student 3, the observer, provides feedback about whether the concept was applied correctly. Student 2 addresses what he/she was thinking during the interchange and the level of comfort with the concept. Then Student 2, in turn, becomes the client; Student 3 the social worker, and Student 1 the observer. This continues several times around until students become more comfortable with the concept and its application.

Concepts are added and the interchanges become increasingly more complex until students are using a number of concepts in the interview exchange and can identify which ones were used and under what circumstances. Generally, I observe from group to group, encouraging, correcting, and listening to what students are doing. Occasionally, I see enough of the same mistakes to stop the class, make corrections, answer questions, and generally redirect the class.

This process serves several purposes. It allows students to immediately put into practice the concepts they are learning in the classroom. It makes them conscious of what they are doing and why. It also provides me with information about where the students are in their learning, what they understand, and in what areas they continue to need explanations and/or practice.

Learning File

In my department, each course syllabus is required to contain a course overview, course objectives, and the course outlined session by session. This conveys the content the department requires. However, in order to engage the learner more completely, as an assignment, I require students to identify and write three to five of their own learning objectives, which they want to meet within the framework of the course. I remind them that objectives should be observable and/or measurable. They are also required to plan and state the manner in which they intend to accomplish each objective and a time frame for their achievement, noting major milestones. In addition to the final product, each student is required to include an analysis of their attainment of their stated objectives. They answer the questions:

- What did you learn?
- What event/information/task had the greatest impact on your attitudes/learning/focus?

- What would you do differently if you had it to do again?

When they are given the assignments, students' tendency is to repeat a variation of course objectives listed on the syllabus. Students are reluctant to risk revealing themselves or to take a chance in making a mistake, as they have been socialized to receive education passively. Once they understand that these objectives should reflect something they want to learn during the course, they are enthusiastic. I do spend time explaining what an objective is, the elements it contains, and how one is worded. I give them a handout with the information I covered in class. I answer any questions students may have, as this is a new task for most of them. Students are asked to bring a draft of their learning objectives to class, usually the second or third class session. I devote one class session to their working in small groups (three to four members each), sharing with others their objectives in order to clarify their intent. Students are usually serious about providing helpful feedback to their classmates. These are then submitted to me for review and feedback. The most frequent problem is that students usually want to do too much. Helping them pare their work to a reasonable size for the time allotted is most of what I am required to do. Generally, students have about 2 months between the time the drafts are due and the due date for the completed assignment.

As I encourage creativity and originality, many of the objectives have produced exciting outcomes. I have received a videotape of interviews with homeless people, a newspaper log of articles related to child abuse in the community, a proposal for the creation of a new community social service agency, and the like.

Minicapstone Experiences

Capstone experiences are designed to be culminating ones at the end of a prescribed course of study. However, these capstone-type or minicapstone experiences could be valuable learning tools for students before they reach the culminating experience. In other words, any strategy that helps and encourages students to integrate rather than encapsulate learning, to progressively add to their fund of knowledge and repertoire of professional behaviors, is one that ultimately prepares them for and adds to the culminating experience.

The minicapstone experience is simply one of adding to any course a final requirement that students analyze their learning during the course or limited set of courses. This may be accomplished by their keeping a journal during the course(s), noting what they have learned, what it means to them, how they are using the knowledge, and how it related to things they have learned in other courses and through other experiences in classes or in their daily lives.

The analysis goes somewhat beyond the log items in that students are asked to generate a short- and long-range learning plan and to determine what needs to be learned in each of those plans, what the current learning means for them, and what knowledge is needed for them to take their next learning steps. If this is to be accomplished over more than one course, then the respective professors must work together to ensure that students are receiving the same instructions and to decide how the final product will be evaluated. I have used the following set of criteria for a number of years and have found them to be worthwhile.

1. Planning and organization: The narrative has an introduction, middle, and conclusion; clear transitions; paragraphs adequately developed with descriptive detail; writer follows a route allowing for orderly progress from one detail to another, one thought to another.

2. Clarity of thought: Thoughts are stated specifically. Vague references are avoided.

3. Depth and specificity of examination: Narrative is sophisticated and maintains focus on topic. Details convey a dominant impression and a consistent point of view.

4. Completeness of assignment: The steps and elements of the assignments are completed in detail and submitted on time.

5. Style: There is interesting, imaginative use of language, concrete nouns, vivid adjectives, strong active verbs, occasional metaphor or simile; the tone is suitable to the purpose and the audience, and jargon is avoided.

6. Grammar and syntax: Sentences convey meaning clearly and grammatically, without sentence fragments or run-on sentences. Sentences are varied in structure and length.

7. Content: Narrative is accurate, comprehensive, and documented appropriately. Extraneous material is avoided and opinions are adequately supported.

8. Spelling and punctuation: Writing is free of errors.

9. Nonsexist language: Nonsexist language is used consistently and throughout the assignment.

Portfolios

Another promising avenue, widely in use already and already explored in Chapter 5 of this volume, is the portfolio. Portfolios as a strategy have the capability of providing a more nearly level playing field, wherein student progress is measured only against itself and not other students, programs, or departments. Portfolios can and are being used in such widely divergent departments as chemistry, classics, and social work and for meeting requirements such as upper division writing requirements.

Bringing It Together

What has been presented here is simply a beginning effort to attend to the teaching and learning of all of the students in my classroom. What the strategies all have in common is continuous feedback for improvement both in teaching and in learning, the paramount aim of assessment. They allow students from different backgrounds to successfully experience higher education in a context that is meaningful to them. The strategies accommodate a variety of worldviews and approaches to life. These strategies and techniques are designed to convey the message that there is a variety of ways of teaching and learning that permit and facilitate intergroup communication, that foster respect for group identity, and that promote transmission of knowledge as a value in and of itself (Banks, 1988, pp. 249-272). However, when all is said and done, education is broader than any one classroom, and many of the problems that all students, especially those from poor, underrepresented, and first-time college-going groups, experience in our universities reflect the problems in the wider society, that is, a general intolerance of people who are different in any way (Banks, 1986, p. 22). The problems in education are too complex to be addressed by single-factor paradigms and simplistic solutions and explanations as we have wont to do in the recent past. We must continue our research investigating the cultural, ethnic, and class differences that make the difference in the teaching/ learning equation and that contribute to subsequent academic success.

Ultimately, taken to its logical conclusion, the changes wrought by equity in teaching, in learning, and in assessment have the potential for changing the face of society itself. Only then can we realize the premise upon which this country was founded, with freedom and justice for all.

References and Resources

Axtell, R. E. (1991). *Gestures*. New York: John Wiley.

Banks, J. A. (1986). Multicultural education: Development, paradigms and goals. In J. A. Banks & J. Lynch (Eds.), *Multicultural education in Western societies* (pp. 21-35). New York: Praeger.

Banks, J. A. (1988). *Multiethnic education: Theory and practice*. Boston: Allyn & Bacon.

Cross, K. P., & Angelo, T. (1988). *Classroom assessment techniques: A handbook for faculty*. University of Michigan: National Center for Research to Improve Postsecondary Teaching and Learning.

Joint Committee for Review of the Master Plan for Higher Education. (1989). *California faces California's future: Education for citizenship in a multicultural democracy.* Sacramento, CA: Joint Publications Office.

Kolodny, A. (1991, February 6). Colleges must recognize students' cognitive styles and cultural backgrounds [Point of View]. *The Chronicle of Higher Education*, p. A44.

Madrid, A. (1990). Diversity and its discontents. *Academe, 76*(6), 14-23.

Maruyama, M. (1974). Paradigmatology and its application to cross-disciplinary, cross-professional, and cross-cultural communication. *Cybernetica, 17*(2), 136-156; *17*(4), 237-282.

Terenzini, P. T. (1989). Assessment with open eyes: Pitfalls in studying student outcomes. *Journal of Higher Education, 60*(6), 644-664.

7 | On Becoming a Mensch or a Mentor

DELORES J. HUFF

The memories of the first day of freshman orientation are so vivid that even now I still experience the same anxiety attack I had walking across the manicured lawns amid the ivy-covered buildings of Tufts University. I had been so terrified, I dashed into a large mausoleum campus building to regain my composure and stood horrified facing a stuffed elephant named Jumbo, a gift from P. T. Barnum. I took this as an ominous symbol. Neither of us really belonged there. After a few minutes, I left and joined a sea of 18-year-olds, all bright and very much better academically prepared than I, a 35-year-old American Indian welfare mother of two.

I was admitted because my social worker, an old, crusty, judgmental, and often sanctimonious woman, had heard of a new Great Society program called WIN (Work Incentive Program, which was originally called WIP, but received such bad public relations that they changed to a more humane sounding acronym). This program, she announced, would send me to school. I was sent to the WIN office and the adviser there told me about a new experimental program at Tufts. They had 10 slots for poor, minority women, experimental because they had rarely admitted anyone beyond the traditional college age for a baccalaureate. I didn't feel very hopeful, especially when I discovered the tuition was $200 less than Harvard. I descended into a dungeon of despair. The WIN social worker remarked that getting in was my problem, getting the tuition paid for was hers. She set up an interview. It was now August.

The interview was with Bea Miller (who is now the president of the Loop College in Chicago), an African American Harvard doctoral student whose brainchild was this experimental program, and that afternoon, with the president of Tufts. The "experiment" was to admit minority women having a track record of being involved in social change (I was an unpaid director of the Boston Indian Center) and give them a first-rate education. Two weeks later I received a letter admitting me, and WIN signed a contract paying for my tuition, books, and $60 a month transportation.

I met with the other nine women at a separate orientation, and with them, one of the most remarkable women I have ever met, Dean Judy Laskaris. In the years to come, it would be Judy who served as mentor, friend, and intellectual sounding board. One day I ventured into Judy's office complaining about some professor who made me rewrite a paper on Indian activists, and we got into an intellectual discourse about language and the differences in the way I used language and what my professor expected of me. She allowed me to mouth off endlessly, but as my rage subsided she entered into the discussion as an interpreter. In that role, I learned the culture of academia, what was expected of me, and how I could either cope or navigate. Years later, with thousands of miles between us and without her ever knowing it, I modeled myself after Judy when students came to my office for advice. Looking back, there seemed to have been four rules she used:

1. She never denied my reality.
2. Her liberalism never extended to patronizing statements such as "knowing how I felt."

3. She never allowed me to use the "differences" in any self-defeating way. My race was not to be used as an excuse not to compete and excel.

4. She empowered me to excel and discover for myself how to balance the rigors of academia with the expectations of my community.

And that brings me to another significant mentor during those years at Tufts, my sociology professor, Alan Ornstein. His door was always open to hours of an intellectual tug-of-war between his gestalt about American Society and mine. His mentoring forte was the ability to integrate my street savvy with the world of ideas.

I mention these people because in spite of the world they knew and came from, they forged an empathic bridge between my ethnic and experiential background and theirs and instilled a sense of empowerment in me where once had been vacant dreams and thundering defeat. They achieved this almost effortlessly, as a true mensch does (an expression meaning a good person, a person who attains joy out of doing good deeds). Alan and Judy, of course, were more than that; they were also mentors. That is they applied the four aforementioned rules, and it was from them that I learned the art of mentoring.

There's not a teacher in the world who doesn't get joy out of the achievement of students. That joy is a significant contributing factor for remaining in the profession as your university puts you through the mind-numbing annual tenure track evaluations. Yet there is a more pragmatic reason for learning how to be an effective mentor. The art of mentoring is the art of communication, which is certainly one measure students and peers use to evaluate effective teaching. Seasoned faculty know students/peers judge them not by what they know, but how well they communicate what they know.

The focus of this chapter is mentoring nontraditional students because this is an area of great concern among both new and seasoned faculty. Who are these nontraditional students?

I define as *nontraditional* students who have had limited options in their lives because of age, sex, race, ethnicity, or class. They have not been socialized to believe college was a possibility in their lives, and for most, their high school experience has reinforced their inadequacies, and they have internalized this negative image.

Nontraditional students have personal courage though, because in spite of enormous self-doubts that they belong in the same world as the traditional student, they filled out the forms, took the SATs, mustered courage, and came onto campus. One other point. For many ethnic minorities, the very act of coming onto campus sets them apart from the community they come from. This separation can often cause painful internal conflict. More about that later.

Although nontraditional students have much in common, the age of the student suggests different strategies for effective mentoring. The following discussion is divided into two segments, the traditional-age minority student and the nontraditional older student.

The Traditional-Age Minority Student

The minority student comes from a barrio, ghetto, or reservation most faculty have studied. But books cannot convey the true reality of their lives, and nothing turns off minority students quicker than for you to express understanding of their milieu. Even within the culture, each individual has selected out those experiences they want to retain in their memory cells so that no two are alike, nor will they respond the same to your earnest mensch endeavors. Your function is to serve as interpreter, to mentor, and in so doing, to empower students who have a lifetime of powerlessness. This is truly the role of a mensch—a person who does good deeds and empowers others to take control of their lives. Here are a few rules you might think about.

❶ **Don't pretend, even to yourself, that you can enter into their world.** Instead, deal with the here and now. This student has come to you for guidance, and sympathy is soothing but tough love is effective. Many American Indian students come to my office frustrated because they must take math or English composition, two subjects which depend heavily on high school preparation. I have had many Indian students with math phobias, and usually they are the ones who excel in writing and research skills. I refused to help them get out of the course, but instead recommend a number of computer programs for daily use until they arrive at a comfort level to take the course. For many it might take a year, but in the end they can master the subject. In any case, for those going on to graduate school, statistics is essential, and they might as well get over their phobia. For students who have a writing phobia, again the lesson is tough love. Make them write it over and over again, go to the writing lab and get help, but on no account should you accept less than what they are capable of producing.

❷ **Demand the same level of excellence from the minority student as from the traditional student.** Many minorities come from exceedingly poor families and must support themselves and their families. It is not unusual for them to put in a 40-hour week at work. This is certainly a legitimate excuse for not completing their work on time. But I believe you need to be firm and flexible—and point out two salient facts. One: They must organize their time to allow for schoolwork because it is a priority, and second, unless they work to the same high level of excellence as their traditional colleagues, they will graduate less prepared for graduate school or professional life. There is no other choice. Work harder. The flexible part is allowing students extra time to complete the project, paper, or study, but it would place them at a disadvantage for their future aspirations if you expect or accept less from them.

❸ **Be on the alert for sources of funding or scholarships because the more students are supported in school, the fewer hours they must work.** Students juggling work and school schedules rarely take the time to find sources of outside funding. For years I have kept a computerized file of unexpected sources for students such as foundations, professional societies, and such and often refer them to these sources. It doesn't take much time, and often can help students to work less and have more time for study.

❹ **Minority students need support systems, and the effective ones are usually the minority campus clubs.** Earlier on, mention was made that some minority students experience conflict about entering college because it separates them from their communities and the norms of their communities. I remember my own conflicts because although I hadn't changed, the Indian community treated me differently, distancing themselves from me, which I found very painful. I was among the first generation of Indians to attend college, and almost no one in the urban Indian community where I lived had education beyond high school. This is the case for many minorities. Experience with Indian students, and my own experience as a student, suggests that the best way for them to cope is to join the American Indian Club on campus or to organize one if one doesn't exist. It is in these clubs students share information about campus life, and this can be invaluable to success. Students share their experiences and this goes a long way to reducing alienation and isolation. Our campus has two American Indian Clubs, and very often students will come to my office with information about a student who is despondent, considering dropping out, or failing. It is then I pick up the phone, get in touch with them (or their parents) and call them into my office. The students in the Indian clubs often pick up on problems before I do.

❺ **Finally, use both push and pull in your mentoring.** When you instinctively know that with a little more encouragement you can get a student to take risks, push. Failure is a familiar friend to many of these students, they've had a lifetime of that. Success entails taking huge risks for those who are afraid to venture out of the familiar. Pulling, on the other hand, is useful when you want them included in intellectual discussions, group interaction—invite them and call them to remind them of an event, lecture, something that pertains to their interest. At least six times a year I invite students to my home for barbecue or pot luck. We sit around and talk and I often have to phone them a couple of times to remind them to come. Once they are there they have an enjoyable time and this gives me a chance to see them outside of my office.

The Older Nontraditional Student

All the aforementioned guidelines apply to the older student, but in all probability it is not strictly academic issues they will bring to your office. You will likely notice the older student in your classroom precisely because they will be the first to articulate a point or defend a position. They rely heavily upon experience and often this can be irritating or even threatening to a neophyte or authoritarian teacher. Use their experience whenever you can. It makes for lively discussions and adds critical thinking to your classroom teaching.

You'll find as these older students come to your office that unlike the younger ones, they need very little motivation. They do need validating, and most of your mentoring skills should be to reinforce or help them broaden the career goals they have in mind and/or encourage them to take more time and fewer courses each term. Older students often present you with personal problems for which you have had very little training. What you have, though, is common sense.

The fact of the matter is the divorce rate for women is extremely high as they approach the final year of their B.A. The degree often signals increased independence to family members and, I am sorry to say, for some husbands, a threat. For many adult women, entry into college often happens as their marriage is already on the decline. (I have never in all these years seen this phenomenon the other way around. Women tend to support their husband's academic aspirations.)

We are beginning to see increasing numbers of adult male enrollments in this structurally changing economy. Whether male or female is enrolled, family stress increases immeasurably with one or both attending college. The loss of income and the time spent studying or writing changes family priorities and affects children as well. It's been my experience that children raise the most fuss but adjust quicker than spouses.

Your role with adult students is to distinguish between normal family issues and those requiring professional counseling. You should have a list of community mental health centers, support groups, and campus counseling programs. When appropriate, ask students to let you set up an initial appointment, and let them know this doesn't mean you will not welcome visits to your office, but that their needs can best be met by an appropriate professional.

Frequently it is necessary to raise the level of expectations for adult students. I had a wonderful analytical adult in my federal-Indian law class who was a natural for law school but had intended to teach high school. His reasoning was that he was in his forties and needed to earn a living. Mine was for him to consider the possibility of three years in law school as an investment in his future. And on more than one occasion I reiterated I think people should enjoy the work they do, life was too tedious otherwise. He went to law school and I have no doubt will do well in a profession he loves.

In this case and in others involving career guidance, I tend to be more directive. Observing student strengths and pointing these out to them often will lead them to unexpected careers.

My classes tend to have a disproportionate percentage of older students, and some I have kept track of over the years. There was Harold, a 70-year-old Chickasaw Indian from Oklahoma who had been a school teacher all his life, retired, and wanted to do a master's thesis on his grandfather, the last old-time chief of his tribe. He had to go into a special master's program, which meant I had to get at least one other department, in this case the anthropology department, to certify his thesis. We had a holy war because the anthropology department felt he had not taken sufficient anthropology courses to qualify, and I had to argue with them that this man had spent all his life understanding firsthand the culture he was writing about. Harold wanted to do a thesis because he said this would serve as an example to other Indians that if he could do it at his age, they could at any age. His thesis is one of the books still in my library.

And then there was Freida, age 50 with 10 children, who wanted to be a nurse. Her math and science background was pretty grim, so I convinced her to audit each course before taking it for credit. It took her longer, but she graduated with both the R.N. and B.S. degrees.

I remembered my own experience at Tufts. It was Judy, my mentor, who convinced me to audit statistics twice before I took it for credit. I found the experience humbling, but in the end, I got an A. Sometimes mentoring older students entails a diplomatic (and humorous—after all the four-year degree is not carved in stone) approach to get them to slow down and take fewer courses because they are not as well-grounded in the foundations as is the traditional student. Be careful to avoid being paternalistic. Older students have strengths not to be taken lightly. They have developed a gestalt about the world and are more comfortable with linking knowledge from different disciplines into a cohesive understanding of subject matter. Because they are so eclectic, they often do not do well on exams. I have worked my classes out so there is a mix of exams, presentations, research, and writing, which allows older students to use their area of strength to good advantage, while at the same time teaching standards are upheld.

In the beginning, students use you as an academic sounding board, and for many that is the relationship that prevails. On the other hand, there are always a few you have developed a special rapport with, and these you follow long after they have taken your course. Mentoring is never a one-time fling, or even a one-year process. Sometimes it takes years before you see any real progress. I have a brilliant student I have been working with since 1985. His math phobia and financial aid problems have slowed him down considerably. He takes a full year of courses one year and the next year off. This year I will finally see him graduate, and I have no doubt (because he is a 4.0 student) he can get into any graduate program he applies for.

The final issue to consider is "letting go." Life is not a map, and students need to find their own shadow. Sometimes students use your good intentions too much, and you must empower them to find their own way. That's not easy when you genuinely enjoy talking with them, but rely upon your instincts as to the proper time to cut the umbilical cord. Empowering means giving them the confidence to find their own solutions. Anything less leaves students as dependent as when they entered college.

I use a rule of thumb. If I've done my job right, they will need me less and less. Structure the time with those who can fly on their own so that they know when to leave the office. Tell them you have something to do, can spare 10 minutes, and explore what it is they came to see you about. Be firm and schedule time in two weeks or later. By that time they have already resolved the problem. And no doubt they will inform you of their decision.

I enjoy mentoring and I think most faculty feel the same way I do. My story at the beginning points out that you don't have to be an ethnic to mentor an ethnic. You don't have to be over 40 to mentor an adult. You have to be a mensch. With that foundation, you can be an effective mentor.

APPENDIX

A Student Profile Questionnaire

San Diego State University
Biology-Microbiology/Environmental Health Major
Spring 1993 Student Profile

Rapid advances in almost all areas of science, changes in vocational interests and opportunities, and financial limitations that must necessarily be placed upon public institutions require that a faculty constantly consider its programs and services to maintain their excellence and currency. The Biology Department continually reviews its curriculum to ensure that the academic needs of both our majors and nonmajors are being met.

An important part of that review requires that the department determine the career goals of its biology, microbiology, and environmental health majors and the financial and other constraints under which our students function. We cannot be all things to all people but we can make a concentrated effort to offer those programs and services which best serve the needs of our students.

To aid the Biology Department faculty in providing the academic programs that you need and that future students will need, we are asking you to complete the attached questionnaire. You will note that no personal identifying information is asked and the information you provide is anonymous. Please be as careful and accurate as possible. If you have completed this questionnaire in another course, please *do not* fill out this copy.

Respectfully,
Carol Barnett, Ph.D.
Chair, Department of Biology

Personal Data

For each of the following questions please fill in the blank or circle the response which applies.

1. How old are you today? _____ years
2. What is your sex?   0   male   1   female
3. Are you married?   0   no   1   yes
4. What languages are spoken in your parent's home? _____

   _____

5. What is your ethnic background?
   0   American Indian
   1   black, non-Hispanic
   2   Chicano, Mexican American
   3   other Hispanic
   4   Asian
   5   Pacific Islander
   6   Filipino
   7   white, non-Hispanic
   8   other
6. Did either of your parents complete a 4-year college?
   0   neither parent
   1   one parent
   2   both parents
7. Where did you attend high school?

   _____
   name of school   city   state
8. Where did you first attend college?
   0   SDSU
   1   local community college
   2   other CSU campus
   3   UC campus
   4   other (please name)
9. When did you enter SDSU?   0 fall   1 spring   19__
10. Why did you decide to attend school at SDSU rather than some other university? (please circle all responses which apply)
    0   recommended by friend/parent/school counselor
    1   financial reasons

    2   local campus
    3   reputation of academic program in biology/microbiology
    4   other (please list) _____

11. Where do you currently live?

    0   dorm
    1   fraternity/sorority house
    2   my parents' home
    3   house or apartment with my spouse
    4   house or apartment where I share rent
    5   other

12. Do you belong to a fraternity or a sorority?   0 No   1 Yes

13. During the fall 1992 semester how much money did your parents contribute to your college education, including tuition, books, rent, food, clothes, car insurance, etc.

    0   None   1   Approximately $ _____

14. During the fall 1992 semester, how much money did you receive in loans which you have to pay back?

    0   None   1   Approximately $ _____

15. During the fall 1992 semester, how much money did you receive in grants which you do not have to pay back?

    0   None   1   Approximately $ _____

16. During the fall 1992 semester, how much money did you receive in scholarships?

    0   None   1   Approximately $ _____

17. During the fall 1992 semester, did you work?

    0   not at all
    1   part of the semester
    2   the entire semester

18. On average, how many hours a week did you work during the fall 1992 semester?

    0 I did not work   1 I worked approximately _____ hours/week

19. How much money did you earn on average by working each month?

    0 I did not work   1 I earned approximately $___ each month

20. Are you working at the present time?   0   No   1   Yes

21. How many hours did you work last week?
    0   I am not working at the present time
    1   I worked ____ hours last week

About Your Academic Studies

22. What is your major?
    0   Biology
    1   Environmental Health
    2   Microbiology
    3   Other (please name) _____

23. Do you intend to return to SDSU for fall semester 1993?
    0   No   1   Yes

24. If you *will not* be returning to SDSU during the fall semester, why are you leaving? (mark all responses which are appropriate) (Skip to Question 25 if you will return in the fall)
    0   I will graduate in May
    1   I will transfer to another university
    2   I plan to work for a period before I continue my education
    3   I can't get the classes I need in a timely fashion
    4   I am moving out of the San Diego area for personal reasons
    5   Other (please explain) _____

25. If you return to SDSU during the fall 1993 semester will you continue in the same major?   0   No   1   Yes

26. How many university credits have you accumulated toward your bachelor's degree?
    0   this is my first semester in college
    1   less than 15
    2   between 16 and 30
    3   between 31 and 60 (sophomore standing)
    4   between 61 and 90 (junior standing)
    5   between 91 and 120 (senior standing)
    6   I am a postbaccalaureate/graduate student

27. How many units did you take during the fall 1992 semester?
    ____ units

28. How many science units are you taking this semester?
    ____ units

29. What science/math courses are you enrolled in this semester?
    1.
    2.
    3.
    4.

30. How many nonscience units are you taking this semester?
    ____

31. Which of the following courses have you taken at SDSU?
    (Circle all appropriate answers.)
    0 Chem 105
    1 Chem 200
    2 Chem 201
    3 Chem 230
    4 Chem 231
    5 Biology 200A (202)
    6 Biology 200B (201)
    7 Biology 215
    8 Math 121
    9 Math 122
    10 Math 150
    11 Physics 180A/182A
    12 Physics 180B/182B
    13 none of the above

32. Which of the upper division core courses have you *completed* at this time?
    0 None
    1 Biology 352 (Genetics)
    2 Chem 361 (Biochemistry)
    3 Biology 354 (Ecology and Evolution)
    4 Biology 356 (Cell Biology)

33. Which upper division biology courses (300 level and above) have you completed as electives at SDSU?
    1.   4.
    2.   5.
    3.   6.

34. Which upper division (300 and above) biology courses do you expect to take as electives prior to graduation?

_____

35. Have you taken any Biology 499 (special studies) units at SDSU?   0 No   1 Yes

36. If you *have taken* Biology 499 units, did you work on a special studies research project with a professor or did you do volunteer work in the community?

    0   work with professor
    1   volunteer
    2   both
    3   I have not taken any Biology 499 units

37. If you *have not taken* any Biology 499 units, do you plan to participate in a special studies project with a professor before you graduate?   0   No   1   Yes

38. Since your arrival at SDSU, have you consulted with a faculty adviser in biology regarding your program of study? (Select all appropriate answers.)

    0   no
    1   yes, I have consulted with Prof. Diehl
    2   yes, I have consulted with Prof. Lewis
    3   yes, I have consulted with Prof. _____
    4   I have consulted with a faculty adviser but I don't remember his/her name

39. In general, do you consult the instructor during office hours when you are having difficulty with a course or with a particular concept in a course?

    0   No
    1   Rarely (1%-24% of the time)
    2   Sometimes (25%-49% of the time)
    3   Frequently (50%-74% of the time)
    4   Usually (75%-99% of the time)
    5   Always

40. In general, what are the biggest problems you have had to overcome when approaching a professor about a problem? (Check all responses which are appropriate.)

    0   I don't want to show my ignorance

1 I don't believe that most professors are interested in helping me
2 I don't know what questions to ask
3 Most professors are not available
4 My work/school schedule is so busy that I don't have time to go to a professor's office hours
5 My professors will not schedule appointments outside their office hours at a time when I am on campus and free
6 I am usually comfortable approaching a faculty member when I have difficulty understanding a concept
7 Other

41. Do you participate in one of the following programs?

0 None
1 HOOP
2 Hughes
3 MARC
4 MBRS
5 REU
6 Other mentoring program _____

42. How many hours did you spend studying last week?
_____ hours

43. How many exams did you prepare for last week?
_____ exams

44. When do you usually start studying for a midterm exam for one of your science courses?

0 the night before the exam
1 2 days before the exam
2 3-4 days before the exam
3 a week before the exam
4 I keep up with the material as it is presented

45. In general, approximately how many hours do you spend preparing for a midterm exam for one of your science courses? _____ hours

46. Approximately what percentage of your class meetings *did you attend* during the fall semester?

0 less than 50% (I missed several class meeting weeks.)
1 51%-75% (I missed a meeting for one of my classes at least once a week.)

    2   76%-90% (I missed a class once every two or three weeks.)

    3   91%-100% (I almost never miss a class.)

47. Where do you do most of your studying?

    0   in the library

    1   at home

    2   at work

    3   other (please list) _____

48. If you miss a class or are late getting to a class, do you make arrangements to get a copy of the lecture notes from another student or the professor who teaches the class?

    0   No

    1   Rarely (1%-24% of the time)

    2   Sometimes (25%-49% of the time)

    3   Frequently (50%-74% of the time)

    4   Usually (75%-99% of the time)

    5   Always

    6   I usually don't get notes from another student, instead I rely on reading the textbook

    7   I get notes from the professor

49. Do you study with a group?

    0   I almost always study alone

    1   I study with a group on a frequent basis (50% of the time)

    2   I frequently study with a group when I am preparing for an exam

    3   I sometimes study with a group when I am preparing for an exam

50. When do you expect to graduate?

    0   fall   1   spring   19____

51. What are your career plans following graduation? (You may circle more than one answer.)

    0   Medical/Dental/Vet School

    1   Graduate School

    2   Recombinant DNA/Biotechnology

    3   Marine Biology

    4   Secondary School Teacher

    5   Ecology/Environmental Studies

    8   Medical Technology

7 Animal Conservation at Zoo/Wild Animal Park/Fish and
Wildlife Service
8 Public Health Department
9 Laboratory Research Technician
10 Sales for Drug Company or Scientific Products Company
11 Plant Sciences (Forestry, Agriculture, Biotech Research)
12 Pharmacy School
13 Museum Collections
14 Other (please name) _____

52. The following question should only be answered by students
who will graduate no later than the end of the *fall 1993
semester*. When you first began as a major in the biological
sciences what were your career goals?
0 Medical/Dental/Vet School
1 Graduate School
2 Recombinant DNA/Biotechnology
3 Marine Biology
4 Secondary School Teacher
5 Ecology/Environmental Studies
6 Medical Technology
7 Animal Conservation at Zoo/Wild Animal Park/Fish and
Wildlife service
8 Public Health Department
9 Laboratory Research Technician
10 Sales for Drug Company or Scientific Products Company
11 Plant Sciences (Forestry, Agriculture, Biotech Research)
12 Pharmacy School
13 Museum Collections
14 Other (please name) _____

About the Authors

Juan C. Gonzalez is Vice President for Student Services at California State University, San Bernardino. In this capacity he oversees the division that houses enrollment services, financial aid, outreach services, services to students with disabilities, international student services, the Student Union, Children's Center, Health Center, and Serrano Village residence halls. He has been a visiting research associate at UCLA's Higher Education Research Institute, studying strategies for assisting low-income and minority students in college. He has served as director of the UCLA Academic Advancement Program. He has consulted for a variety of educational agencies, including the California Postsecondary Commission and the Tomas Rivera Center in Claremont, California. He is a past chair of the American Association for Higher Education's Hispanic Caucus and a current executive board member of the American Association of University Administrators.

Olita Dargan Harris is Associate Professor in the School of Social Work, Associate Dean of the Division of Undergraduate Studies, and Acting Associate Dean of the College of Health and Human Services at San Diego State University. She chairs the University Assessment Committee and has served as coordinator and chair of two CSU system-wide conferences on student outcomes assessment. Her experience includes assessing institutional effectiveness through participation in specialized accreditation, academic program reviews, and institution accreditation. She has made numerous presentations on institutional effectiveness, and on curriculum building and classroom assessment in a multicultural setting.

Delores J. Huff is Professor of American Indian Studies at California State University, Fresno. She serves as advisor to two American Indian Clubs at Fresno State, and to Indian and non Indian students working with Indian tribes and organizations. She was a delegate from California to the White House Conference on Indian Education and has consulted for the Office of Indian Education, Bureau of Indian Affairs, and the Office of Indian Health. She has participated in the Full Circle organization, a national consortium of college and universities which seeks to recruit Indian students into graduate school. She has been consultant/evaluator for the Lummi Tribe in Washington State and the Ft. Belknap Indian reservation in Montana. She was cofounder and education director of the Boston Indian Center and was appointed by the White House to the National Advisory Board for Vocational and Technical Education. She has presented papers on her work to international audiences, and has been guest lecturer at the Universities of Genoa and Turino and Opporte (Portugal).

Ann M. Johns is Professor of Linguistics and Writing Studies at San Diego State University, where she directed the Writing Across the Curriculum/Critical Thinking Program (WAC) for several years. She is academic coordinator of the SDSU University Seminar, a cooperative Faculty/Student Affairs program designed to initiate freshmen into campus culture and prepare them for academic success. She designed and has taught in a model integrated freshman program for diverse students in which academic reading and writing, content, and counseling are merged to promote transfer of skills, student motivation, and retention. She serves on the College of Arts and Letters Diversity Initiatives Committee and was co-coordinator of the CSU Institute for Teaching and Learning Seminar on English as a Second Language. She worked with faculty from other CSU campuses to found an ongoing English for Academic Purposes (EAP) Group for teachers of linguistically diverse students. She travels widely, in the United States and abroad, to consult with universities and teachers about EAP issues.

Ray Lou is Associate Academic Vice President for Undergraduate Studies and Professor of Asian American Studies at San Jose State University, where he oversees all major and minor programs, special majors, and the Honors program, and administers the General Education Program. He is also responsible for the campus's educational equity programs and policies including recruitment of underrepresented students, admissions, academic support services, faculty mentoring, and advising. He is currently involved in two major research projects, one on race and ethnic relations among college students the other dealing with the academic success of underrepresented students. He has extensive experience in program planning and curriculum development.

Helen Roberts is Director of Academic Programs and Support for the twenty campus California State University System, where she works with faculty throughout the state to improve the educational program for California's diverse students. She oversees the Office of Extended Education, the CSU Institute for Teaching and Learning, and the California Academic Partnership Program (with K-12 schools). Prior to joining CSU, she was Director of the Office of Community Development and Public Service for the American Association of State Colleges and Universities, and served as Associate Director of the 1986 National Commission on the Role and Future of State Colleges and Universities. She is a specialist in multicultural curriculum. She has worked in elementary and secondary education as Director of Curriculum and Evaluation for the Northwest

Arctic School District in Northwest Alaska, where she also taught courses in curriculum development and culture and education for the University of Alaska.

Otis L. Scott is Professor of Government and Ethnic Studies at California State University, Sacramento. For the past fourteen years he has served as the Coordinator of the Ethnic Studies Center. For many years He has actively participated in curriculum development projects at both secondary and post-secondary levels. He was codirector of the project "Using Ethnic Literature to Teach Critical Thinking Skills," which was sponsored by the California Academic Partnership Program (CAPP). He is codirector of "Beyond the Canon," a university-based curriculum development project which helps faculty include multicultural content in general education courses. He is a member of the Executive Council of the National Association for Ethnic Studies, and is completing a book on ethnic group experience in the United States.